P9-BYJ-274

GEORGE FOREMAN®

RECIPES!

Pascoe Publishing, Inc.
Rocklin, California

ISBN: 1-929862-32-6

03   04   05   06   10   9   8   7   6   5   4   3   2   1

TABLE OF CONTENTS

CHAPTER 1

Introduction to Your George Foreman® Lean Mean Contact Roasting Machine

Welcome to the wonderful world of contact roasting! Roasting used to require demanding food preparation, long hours of cooking and an overheated kitchen. With the introduction of the George Foreman® Lean Mean Contact Roasting Machine, you now have the quick and easy answer to incredibly delicious roasting in a fraction of the time.

Roasting brings out the best of large cuts of beef, whole chicken, game hens, stuffed fish fillets and a wide variety of vegetables and fruit. The heat of the George Foreman® Lean Mean Contact Roasting Machine combined with the unique contact roasting design elements produce the most incredibly moist and flavorful roasted beef, poultry and seafood imaginable.

When you use your George Foreman® Lean Mean Contact Roasting Machine for the first time, carefully read the Owner's Manual for cooking and safety instructions. In addition, you'll find the following hints helpful each time you use your George Foreman® Lean Mean Contact Roasting Machine.

★ Use caution when opening and closing the George Foreman® Lean Mean Contact Roasting Machine. Wear oven mitts when placing the Baking Pan into the Contact Roaster or whenever you remove foods from the Contact Roaster.

★ Watch the drip tray carefully when roasting large cuts of meat or poultry and replace or drain and replace as needed. Exercise caution and care when moving the drip trays to avoid spilling the hot liquids. It is best to allow the liquids to cool prior to removing the drip tray from under the Contact Roaster.

★ Do not use metal utensils in the George Foreman® Lean Mean Contact Roasting Machine. The inside of the Contact Roaster has been coated with a special nonstick coating and metal will scratch or mar the surface. Use long-handled wooden or plastic utensils only for long-term care of your Contact Roaster.

★ Test meats, poultry and seafood to determine that they are cooked to the proper temperatures prior to serving. Use an internal meat

50 Great George Foreman® Lean Mean Contact Roasting Machine Recipes!

5

thermometer and always cook beef to a minimum of 145°F, pork to a minimum of 160°F and poultry to 180°F to eliminate harmful bacteria in foods. Place the meat thermometer in the thickest part of the meat or poultry away from any bones.

★ Because the George Foreman® Lean Mean Contact Roasting Machine quickly roasts beef, use cuts of beef that can be tenderized by the addition of broth or juices such as beef tenderloin or tri-tip roasts. Cross rib roasts and cuts of sirloin are also excellent when prepared in the Contact Roaster. Remove all visible fat before roasting.

★ Substitute light au jus gravies and natural broths for heavy, fat-laden gravy. The unique properties of the George Foreman® Lean Mean Contact Roasting Machine allows the fat to drip away, leaving the moist and tender flavor in the meat, poultry and seafood for you to enjoy.

★ Fish and seafood should be opaque or flake easily with a fork when done. Adjust cooking times as needed to fully cook fish to proper temperatures.

★ Contact Roasting is fun! Enjoy your George Foreman® Lean Mean Contact Roasting Machine by using it for a wide variety of your own recipes. Experiment with the times needed for cooking by using the recipes in this cookbook as a basic guide.

★ Rice and grains cook very well in the George Foreman® Lean Mean Contact Roasting Machine. You can place the water, rice or other grains and salt in the Contact Roaster and enjoy the fact that your grains will be cooked to perfection every time. Risotto recipes work especially well in the Contact Roaster, as the moist heat preserves the softened texture of the rice.

★ Use your George Foreman® Lean Mean Contact Roasting Machine to steam your favorite vegetables. The Wire Rack can be used as a steaming rack for cut vegetables or, in the inverted position, to steam larger vegetables such as artichokes. Vegetables retain more nutrients and are tender-crisp when prepared in the Contact Roaster, so you can prepare squash, potatoes, peppers, carrots, beets, onions–in fact, just about any vegetable–and get outstanding results.

CHAPTER 2

Great Appetizers & Snacks

Whether you are preparing appetizers for a special evening meal or hunting for a quick snack during the day, the recipes inside this chapter offer a wide variety of tempting choices. You'll find that preparation is easy, cooking is fast and clean-up is a breeze with your George Foreman® Lean Mean Contact Roasting Machine.

The Baking Pan included with your Contact Roaster is a perfect tool for roasting, steaming or baking creative appetizers. Try *Three Cheese & Chive Mushrooms* and *Roasted Corn & Red Peppers with Baked Tortilla Chips*. For a taste of the Orient, try the *Crab-Filled Wonton*. The versatility of your George Foreman® Lean Mean Contact Roasting Machine is remarkable and, when partnered with the George Foreman® Lean Mean Fat Reducing Grilling Machine, you have the quick and easy answer to appetizers and snacks of all kinds!

Three Cheese & Chive Mushrooms

20 medium white button mushrooms,
cleaned and dried, stems removed
16 oz. fat free cream cheese, softened
1/2 c. lowfat mozzarella cheese, shredded

1/4 c. Parmesan cheese, grated
2 T. fresh chives, finely minced
1 t. black pepper

*12 quart Contact Roaster: With a small spoon, scoop out the meat of each mushroom. Set the caps aside and chop the mushrooms finely. Place in a medium mixing bowl and add the cream cheese, mozzarella cheese, Parmesan cheese, chives and black pepper. Mix thoroughly to blend.

Preheat the Contact Roaster. Fill each mushroom cap with the cheese spread and arrange the mushrooms in the Baking Pan. The sides of the mushrooms will touch, but should not be overly crowded. Using oven mitts, place the Baking Pan in the Contact Roaster and set the Timer for 15 to 20 minutes. The mushrooms will be done when the caps are browned and the cheese spread is melted and warm. Serve while warm. Serves 10.

*4 quart Contact Roaster: Roast one-half of the mushrooms in the Contact Roaster as directed and cover the remaining mushrooms with plastic wrap. Place in the refrigerator until the first half of the mushrooms are cooked. Repeat the cooking process with the remaining mushrooms.

NUTRITIONAL ANALYSIS:

Calories: 62
Total fat: 1 g
Saturated fat: <1 g
% calories from fat: 11
Carbohydrates: 5 g
Protein: 9 g
Cholesterol: 2 mg
Sodium: 333 mg

Spinach & Green Onion Vegetable Roll-Ups

10 oz. frozen chopped spinach, thawed and squeezed dry
1 c. canned artichokes, packed in water, drained
1/2 c. black olives, chopped
1/4 c. green onions, thinly sliced
8 oz. nonfat cream cheese, softened

1/2 c. nonfat mayonnaise
1 t. black pepper
dash bottled hot sauce
4 9-inch lowfat flour tortillas
nonfat cooking spray

NUTRITIONAL ANALYSIS:

Calories: 103
Total fat: 1 g
Saturated fat: <1 g
% calories from fat: 11
Carbohydrates: 17 g
Protein: 6 g
Cholesterol: 0 mg
Sodium: 543 mg

*12 quart Contact Roaster: Mix together in a medium mixing bowl, the spinach, artichokes, olives and onions. Toss to mix well. Add the cream cheese, mayonnaise, pepper and hot sauce. Blend well.

To assemble, place 1 tortilla on a flat working surface. Cover with one-fourth of the spinach spread, leaving a ½-inch margin around the edge of the tortilla. Roll up the tortilla and tightly cover in plastic wrap. Repeat with the remaining roll-ups. Refrigerate for 1 hour.

Preheat the Contact Roaster. Unwrap the tortillas and cut into slices 1-inch thick. Place the slices, cut side down, in the Baking Pan and use oven mitts to place the Baking Pan in the Contact Roaster. Cook the roll-ups for 8 to 10 minutes, or until warm and softened. Makes 36 pieces.

*4 quart Contact Roaster: Place one-half of the roll-ups in the Baking Pan and cook as directed. Repeat with the remaining roll-ups.

Hot Sauced Bayou Shrimp

4 lbs. uncooked large shrimp, peeled and
    deveined, tails removed
3 cloves garlic, minced
juice 2 lemons
1/4 c. vegetable oil

1 T. bottled hot sauce
1 1/2 t. chili powder
2 T. tomato paste
1 t. salt

*12 quart Contact Roaster: Place the shrimp in a large, sealable plastic bag. Whisk together the garlic, lemon juice, oil, hot sauce, chili powder, tomato paste and salt and pour over the shrimp. Mix the shrimp with the sauce, coating each piece thoroughly and refrigerate the shrimp for 1 hour.

Preheat the Contact Roaster. Place the shrimp in the Baking Pan and discard the sauce.

Using oven mitts, place the Baking Pan in the Contact Roaster and set the Timer for 20 to 35 minutes. The shrimp will be done when they are completely pink and opaque throughout. Serve while hot. Serves 20.

*4 quart Contact Roaster: Use 2 pounds of shrimp and decrease the recipe ingredients by half. Roast as directed. Serves 10.

NUTRITIONAL ANALYSIS:

Calories: 124
Total fat: 4 g
Saturated fat: 2 g
% calories from fat: 32
Carbohydrates: 2 g
Protein: 19 g
Cholesterol: 137 mg
Sodium: 257 mg

Crab-Filled Wonton

1 1/2 lbs. fresh crabmeat, picked and
    cleaned or use frozen, thawed crabmeat
6 green onions, thinly sliced
2 ribs celery, finely minced
2 carrots, peeled and finely minced
3 T. rice vinegar

1/4 c. nonfat mayonnaise
1/4 c. nonfat sour cream
1 t. fresh lemon juice
24 wonton rounds
1 egg, beaten
nonfat cooking spray

*12 quart Contact Roaster: Combine the crabmeat, onions, celery, carrots, vinegar, mayonnaise, sour cream and lemon juice and blend well. Place one wonton on a flat surface and scoop one teaspoonful of crab onto one-half of the round. Brush the edges of the wonton with egg and fold one-half of the wonton over the filling. Press the edges of the wonton with your fingertips to seal. Repeat with the remaining wonton.

Preheat the Contact Roaster. Coat the Baking Pan with cooking spray and place the wonton in the Baking Pan with the sealed edge on top, flattening the bottom of the wonton slightly in the Pan. Using oven mitts, place the Baking Pan in the Contact Roaster and set the Timer for 15 to 20 minutes. The wonton will be done when the crab filling is cooked through and the wonton are very soft. Serves 12.

*4 quart Contact Roaster: Decrease the ingredients by half and cook for 10 to 15 minutes as directed above. Serves 6.

NUTRITIONAL ANALYSIS:

Calories: 160
Total fat: 4 g
Saturated fat: 1 g
% calories from fat: 24
Carbohydrates: 16 g
Protein: 14 g
Cholesterol: 59 mg
Sodium: 343 mg

50 Great George Foreman® Lean Mean Contact Roasting Machine Recipes!

Roasted Corn & Red Peppers with Blue Tortilla Chips

3 c. fresh corn kernels (you may substitute
    frozen or canned, drained corn)
1 jalapeño pepper, seeded and minced
1 red bell pepper, cored, seeded and
    chopped
1/2 c. white onion, chopped

1 T. extra virgin olive oil
1 c. egg substitute
salt and black pepper to taste
1/4 c. Parmesan cheese, finely grated
8 oz. baked blue corn tortilla chips

*12 quart Contact Roaster: Preheat the Contact Roaster. Place the corn, peppers and onion in the Baking Pan and drizzle with the olive oil. Using oven mitts, place the Baking Pan in the Contact Roaster and set the Timer for 10 minutes. Cook and stir once with a plastic spatula while roasting. Remove the Baking Pan from the Contact Roaster and pour the egg substitute over the vegetables and sprinkle with the salt and pepper to taste. Sprinkle evenly with the cheese. Place the Baking Pan in the Contact Roaster and set the Timer for 20 minutes. Remove when the egg substitute is set and serve with the tortilla chips. Serves 8.

*4 quart Contact Roaster: Decrease the ingredients by half. Cook the corn, peppers and onion for 10 minutes as directed above. Cook the vegetables and egg for a total of 10 minutes as directed above. Serves 4.

NUTRITIONAL ANALYSIS:
Calories: 233
Total fat: 5 g
Saturated fat: 1 g
% calories from fat: 20
Carbohydrates: 38 g
Protein: 9 g
Cholesterol: 2 mg
Sodium: 580 mg

CHAPTER 3

Great Vegetables, Side Dishes & Desserts

A perfectly prepared meal includes exciting, innovative vegetables and side dishes and the George Foreman® Lean Mean Contact Roasting Machine quickly roasts, steams and bakes your food. To prepare healthy steamed vegetables, place 2 cups of water in the Baking Pan. Place the Wire Rack inside the baking pan and cover with the cleaned and cut vegetables of your choice. Cover and steam for up to 75 minutes, depending on the vegetable. Check the vegetables frequently. They should be tender-crisp when ready to serve. If you are using the 4-quart Contact Roaster, prepare about 3 cups of your choice of vegetables and place them in the Baking Pan. Add approximately ¼ to ½-cup of water and cook until tender-crisp.

Side dishes delight family and guests alike. A simple chop, steak or grilled chicken breast prepared in the George Foreman® Lean Mean Grilling Machine can be perfectly accented by any of the side dishes in this chapter. The following recipes are designed to be a nutritious, yet satisfying addition to your meal. Try *Prosciutto & Parmesan Golden Steamed Rice, Herb & Bacon-Stuffed Maui Onions* and *Baby Spinach Salad with Asparagus & Sesame Cilantro Dressing.*

You will be surprised and pleased with the George Foreman® Lean Mean Contact Roasting Machine when it comes to making desserts. Fruits bake to a rich mellow flavor and desserts such as crisps, crumbles and buckles bake easily. Try our *Poached Anjou Pears in Ginger Syrup, Duo Strawberry Galette* and the tempting *A "Lighter" Chocolate Cake.* You and your family will be pleased with the results.

Sweet Roasted Milano Vegetables

1 large portobello mushroom, cleaned and roughly diced

1 c. porcini mushrooms, cleaned and thickly sliced

3 large carrots, peeled and sliced 1/2-inch thick

1 large purple onion, peeled and sliced 1/4-inch thick

3 zucchini squash, cleaned, trimmed and sliced 1/2-inch thick

2 T. balsamic vinegar

2 T. extra virgin olive oil

1 T. fresh flat-leaf parsley, minced

pinch sugar

NUTRITIONAL ANALYSIS:

Calories: 86

Total fat: 5 g

Saturated fat: 1 g

% calories from fat: 48

Carbohydrates: 10 g

Protein: 2 g

Cholesterol: 0 mg

Sodium: 17 mg

*12 quart Contact Roaster: Preheat the Contact Roaster. Place the mushrooms, carrots, onion and squash in the Baking Pan. Whisk together in a small bowl, the vinegar, oil, parsley and sugar. Pour the vinaigrette over the vegetables and turn to coat. Using oven mitts, place the Baking Pan in the Contact Roaster and set the Timer for 40 minutes. Test the vegetables with a fork. If it pierces the vegetables easily, the vegetables are ready. If not, continue cooking for an additional 5 to 10 minutes. Serve immediately. Serves 6.

*4 quart Contact Roaster: Decrease the ingredients by half and roast the vegetables for 20 to 30 minutes as directed above. Serves 3 to 4.

Herb & Bacon-Stuffed Walla Walla Onions

6 Walla Walla onions, peeled
5 c. dry peasant-style bread, cut into small
   cubes
1/2 c. chicken broth
1 T. extra virgin olive oil
3 cloves garlic, minced

3 slices turkey bacon, cooked and crumbled
1/3 c. Parmesan cheese, grated
2 T. fresh parsley, minced
1 1/2 t. salt
1 t. black pepper

*12 quart Contact Roaster: Preheat the Contact Roaster. Cut part of the bottom off of each onion so that it will stand in the Baking Pan. Cut across the top of the onion to expose the inner core. Pull out the inner pieces of onion, leaving a ¼–inch wall of onion layers. Dice the inner layers of the onions. In a large bowl, mix together the onions, bread cubes, broth, oil, garlic, bacon, cheese, parsley, salt and pepper. Toss well to combine.

Pack each onion with the herb stuffing and place the onions in the Baking Pan. Using oven mitts, place the Baking Pan in the Contact Roaster and set the Timer for 30 to 45 minutes. The onions will be done when soft to the touch and lightly browned. Serves 6.

*4 quart Contact Roaster: Substitute 3 to 4 onions and decrease the remaining ingredients by half. Roast the onions for 30 minutes and test for doneness as directed above. Serves 4.

NUTRITIONAL ANALYSIS:

Calories: 230
Total fat: 7 g
Saturated fat: 2 g
% calories from fat: 27
Carbohydrates: 34 g
Protein: 8 g
Cholesterol: 9 mg
Sodium: 1070 mg

Baby Spinach Salad with Asparagus & Sesame Cilantro Dressing

3 lbs. fresh tender asparagus, trimmed to no more than 6 inches long

6 c. baby spinach leaves, cleaned and crisped in the refrigerator

1 c. romaine lettuce leaves, cleaned, torn and crisped in the refrigerator

2 large ripe tomatoes, seeded and diced

3 T. sweet onion, minced

3 cloves garlic, minced

2 T. fresh cilantro, chopped

2 t. sesame oil

salt and pepper to taste

NUTRITIONAL ANALYSIS:
Calories: 90
Total fat: 2 g
Saturated fat: <1 g
% calories from fat: 19
Carbohydrates: 15 g
Protein: 9 g
Cholesterol: 0 mg
Sodium: 61 mg

*12 quart Contact Roaster: Do not preheat the Contact Roaster. Pour 2 cups of water into the Baking Pan and place the Baking Pan in the Contact Roaster. Place the Wire Rack in the Baking Pan and arrange the asparagus on the rack, layering as evenly as possible. Cover and set the Timer for 25 to 35 minutes. Check the asparagus when the Timer goes off. The asparagus will be tender-crisp when done. Remove from the Wire Rack with a slotted plastic spatula and cool slightly.

To assemble the salad, toss together the spinach, romaine, tomatoes, onion, garlic and cilantro. Portion the salad onto 6 individual plates. Cover each serving with the asparagus and drizzle with the sesame oil. Sprinkle with salt and pepper to taste. Serve immediately. Serves 6.

*4 quart Contact Roaster: Decrease the ingredients by half and cook the asparagus in the Baking Pan in ½ cup of water for 20 to 25 minutes, or until tender-crisp. Serves 3 to 4.

Creole Red Rice & Black Bean Salad

2 c. long grain white rice
3 c. water
1 3/4 c. tomato juice
2 - 15 oz. cans black beans, drained
3 medium tomatillos, diced
1 green bell pepper, seeded and diced
4 green onions, chopped

4 oz. jar fire-roasted peppers, drained
1/2 c. nonfat sour cream
1/2 c. nonfat mayonnaise
2 T. lowfat milk
1/4 c. fresh cilantro, chopped
salt and pepper to taste

*12 quart Contact Roaster: Spread the rice in the Baking Pan and slowly add the water and tomato juice. Place the Baking Pan in the Contact Roaster and set the Timer for 70 minutes. When the rice is done, remove from the Contact Roaster and cool for 15 minutes.

In a medium mixing bowl, toss together the black beans, tomatillos, pepper and onions.

Process in a blender the fire-roasted peppers, sour cream, mayonnaise and milk until smooth. To assemble the salad, spread the cooked rice on a large serving platter and cover with the black beans and vegetables. Pour the dressing over all and serve at room temperature. Serves 6 to 8.

*4 quart Contact Roaster: Decrease the ingredients by half and cook the rice for 45 minutes. Serves 4.

NUTRITIONAL ANALYSIS:
Calories: 280
Total fat: 1 g
Saturated fat: <1 g
% calories from fat: 2
Carbohydrates: 62 g
Protein: 9 g
Cholesterol: 3 mg
Sodium: 774 mg

50 Great George Foreman® Lean Mean Contact Roasting Machine Recipes!

19

Roasted Yukon Gold Potatoes with Rosemary

6 Yukon Gold potatoes, cleaned
1 1/2 t. salt
1 t. freshly ground black pepper

2 T. extra virgin olive oil
2 T. fresh rosemary, snipped
1 T. Italian flat-leaf parsley, minced

NUTRITIONAL ANALYSIS:
Calories: 76
Total fat: 4 g
Saturated fat: 1 g
% calories from fat: 40
Carbohydrates: 9 g
Protein: 3 g
Cholesterol: 0 mg
Sodium: 448 mg

*12 quart Contact Roaster: Preheat the Contact Roaster. Cut the potatoes into eighths and place in the Baking Pan. Sprinkle the salt and pepper over the potatoes and drizzle with the oil. Cover the potatoes with the rosemary and parsley. Using oven mitts, place the Baking Pan in the Contact Roaster and set the Timer for 70 minutes. A fork will easily pass through the meat of the potatoes when done. Roast for an additional 10 minutes, if needed. Remove the potatoes from the Contact Roaster and serve immediately. Serves 6 to 8.

*4 quart Contact Roaster: Substitute 4 potatoes, 1 t. salt, ½ t. black pepper and 1 tablespoon each of the olive oil and rosemary. Sprinkle with 2 t. Italian parsley. Roast for 60 minutes as directed above. Serves 4.

Prosciutto & Parmesan Golden Steamed Rice

2 c. long grain white rice
5 c. hot water
1 1/2 t. salt
1 t. unsalted butter
1/4 c. green onions, chopped
4 cloves garlic, minced

1 T. fresh oregano, minced
4 oz. prosciutto, chopped
1/4 c. lowfat Parmesan cheese, grated
salt and freshly ground black pepper to taste
nonfat cooking spray

*12 quart Contact Roaster: Coat the Baking Pan with cooking spray and pour the rice into the Pan. Spread the rice evenly in the Pan. Add the water and salt and dot with the butter. Place the Baking Pan in the Contact Roaster and turn on the Roaster. Set the Timer to 60 minutes.

When the Timer goes off, open the Contact Roaster using oven mitts. Sprinkle the green onions, garlic, oregano, prosciutto and Parmesan cheese over the rice and mix in evenly using a plastic spatula. Cover and set the Timer for 10 minutes. Steam until done and serve while warm. Serves 8.

*4 quart Contact Roaster: Decrease all of the ingredients by half and steam the rice for a total of 45 minutes. Serves 4.

NUTRITIONAL ANALYSIS:

Calories: 219
Total fat: 3 g
Saturated fat: 1 g
% calories from fat: 12
Carbohydrates: 39 g
Protein: 8 g
Cholesterol: 9 mg
Sodium: 886 mg

Mediterranean Tomato & Herb Couscous

2 1/2 c. hot vegetable broth
1 clove garlic, minced
1/2 t. ground cumin
1 t. fresh oregano, minced
1 T. Italian flat-leaf parsley, minced
1 c. quick-cooking couscous

1 large ripe tomato, chopped
3 green onions, sliced
1 cucumber, peeled and chopped
2 T. fresh lemon juice
1/4 c. extra virgin olive oil
1/2 c. feta cheese, crumbled

NUTRITIONAL ANALYSIS:

Calories: 296
Total fat: 15 g
Saturated fat: 4 g
% calories from fat: 45
Carbohydrates: 33 g
Protein: 8 g
Cholesterol: 13 mg
Sodium: 678 mg

*12 quart Contact Roaster: Pour the hot broth into the Baking Pan and add the garlic, cumin, oregano, parsley and couscous. Place the Baking Pan in the Contact Roaster and set the Timer for 15 minutes. When done, remove the couscous from the Contact Roaster and spoon onto a serving platter. Top with the tomato, onions and cucumber. Whisk together the lemon juice and olive oil and drizzle over the vegetables and couscous. Sprinkle the feta cheese over all and serve immediately. Serves 4 to 5.

*4 quart Contact Roaster: Cook as directed above.

Soft Polenta with Chanterelle Mushroom Sauce

4 1/2 c. hot water
2 c. yellow cornmeal
1 1/2 t. salt
1/2 t. black pepper
2 T. lowfat margarine, cut into pieces
4 oz. chanterelle mushrooms, cleaned and sliced

1 1/2 c. beef broth
1/4 c. white onion, minced
1 1/2 T. cornstarch
1/3 c. evaporated skim milk
1 t. salt
1/2 t. black pepper

*12 quart Contact Roaster: Pour the hot water into the Baking Pan and sprinkle the cornmeal over the top. Add the salt and pepper and stir to mix well. Dot the top of the cornmeal with small pieces of the margarine and place the Baking Pan in the Contact Roaster. Close and set the Timer for 30 minutes.

Using oven mitts, remove the polenta, and cool in the Baking Pan on a wire rack for 20 minutes. Combine the mushrooms, broth and onion in a small saucepan and heat to a low boil. Mix together the cornstarch and evaporated milk and add salt and pepper to taste. Slowly pour the cornstarch and milk into the broth and stir until the sauce is thickened.

To serve, spoon the soft polenta onto individual plates and lightly sauce. Serves 8.

*4 quart Contact Roaster: Decrease all of the ingredients by half and cook for 20 to 30 minutes. Prepare the sauce as directed above. Serves 4.

NUTRITIONAL ANALYSIS:
Calories: 185
Total fat: 3 g
Saturated fat: 1 g
% calories from fat: 14
Carbohydrates: 35 g
Protein: 5 g
Cholesterol: <1 mg
Sodium: 1477 mg

Poached Anjou Pears in Ginger Syrup

8 small Anjou pears, washed
2 small pieces gingerroot, finely grated
4 small pieces crystallized ginger, finely
    chopped

1/2 c. light corn syrup
2 c. water

*12 quart Contact Roaster: Cut a small slice from the bottom of each pear so that the pears will stand upright. Place the pears in the Baking Pan. In a small saucepan, combine the fresh gingerroot, crystallized ginger, corn syrup and water. Bring to a rolling boil and simmer for 2 minutes. Carefully pour the ginger syrup evenly over the top of each pear, using all of the syrup.

Preheat the Contact Roaster. Using oven mitts, place the Baking Pan in the Contact Roaster and set the Timer for 90 to 110 minutes. Test the pears to determine if they are done by pressing gently against the skin. The pear should be very tender when ready. To serve, scoop each pear into individual serving dishes and top with any remaining sauce. Serves 8.

*4 quart Contact Roaster: Select 4 pears and decrease the remaining ingredients by half. Cook for 60 to 80 minutes as directed above. Serves 4.

Sweet Toffee Roasted Apples

8 tart baking apples, peeled and cored
1/4 c. butter or margarine, softened
1/2 c. hard toffee candies, crushed

2 oz. almonds, chopped
1/4 c. powdered sugar

*12 quart Contact Roaster: Cut a thin slice from the bottom of each apple so that it will stand upright in the Baking Pan. Place the apples in the Baking Pan. Mix together in a small bowl, the butter, candies, almonds and powdered sugar. Pack the center of each apple with the toffee stuffing.

Preheat the Contact Roaster. Using oven mitts, place the Baking Pan into the Contact Roaster and set the Timer for 35 to 45 minutes. The apples will be ready when they are just tender. Serves 8.

*4 quart Contact Roaster: Use 4 apples and decrease the remaining ingredients by half. Cook for 25 to 35 minutes as directed above. Serves 4.

NUTRITIONAL ANALYSIS:
Calories: 267
Total fat: 12 g
Saturated fat: 5 g
% calories from fat: 39
Carbohydrates: 41 g
Protein: 2 g
Cholesterol: 20 mg
Sodium: 90 mg

Farmhouse Raspberry & Apple Crumble

8 tart baking apples, peeled, cored and
    thinly sliced
2 c. fresh raspberries (you may substitute
    frozen, thawed raspberries, if desired)
2 T. sugar
1 c. all-purpose flour

1/3 c. sugar
2 t. ground cinnamon
1/2 c. butter or margarine, softened
1/2 c. quick-cooking or regular rolled oats
1/4 c. walnuts, chopped
nonfat cooking spray

NUTRITIONAL ANALYSIS:
Calories: 310
Total fat: 12 g
Saturated fat: 6 g
% calories from fat: 33
Carbohydrates: 51 g
Protein: 3 g
Cholesterol: 25 mg
Sodium: 94 mg

*12 quart Contact Roaster: Coat the Baking Pan with nonstick cooking spray and preheat the Contact Roaster. Combine the apples and raspberries in a medium mixing bowl and toss with the 2 tablespoons of sugar.

In another bowl, combine the flour, remaining sugar and cinnamon. Cut in the butter with a pastry blender or 2 knives until the mixture resembles crumbs and the butter is evenly distributed. Stir in the oats and walnuts.

Spoon the apples and raspberries into the Baking Pan. Scatter the crumbled mixture over the fruit, covering it evenly. Using oven mitts, place the Baking Pan in the Contact Roaster and set the Timer for 60 to 70 minutes. The dessert is done when the fruit is very soft and tender and heated throughout. Serves 10.

*4 quart Contact Roaster: Use 4 baking apples and decrease the remaining ingredients by half. Cook for 40 to 50 minutes as directed above. Serves 5 to 6.

Duo Strawberry Galette

9 oz. frozen puff pastry, thawed
3 c. fresh strawberries, cleaned and hulled
1 T. unsalted butter, cut into small pieces
2 T. sugar

3 T. strawberry jelly
1 T. water
pinch salt

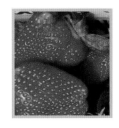

*12 quart Contact Roaster: Place the thawed puff pastry in the Baking Pan and loosely arrange in the shape of a circle. Place the strawberries with the hull side down over the pastry in a circular fashion, completely covering the pastry except for a border of about 1–inch around the edges. Fold in the edges of the pastry over the top of the strawberries on the outer edges. Dot the strawberries with the butter and sprinkle with the sugar.

Preheat the Contact Roaster. Using oven mitts, place the Baking Pan in the Contact Roaster and set the Timer for 40 to 50 minutes, or until the fruit is soft. Remove the galette and cool on a rack for 20 minutes.

While the galette cools, heat the strawberry jelly, water and salt in a small saucepan. Heat and stir until the sauce starts to simmer. Remove from the heat and brush the strawberry galette with the glaze, covering the strawberries evenly. Serves 8.

*4 quart Contact Roaster: Decrease all of the ingredients by half and cook for 30 to 40 minutes as directed above. Serves 4.

NUTRITIONAL ANALYSIS:

Calories: 237
Total fat: 4 g
Saturated fat: 4 g
% calories from fat: 52
Carbohydrates: 26 g
Protein: 3 g
Cholesterol: 4 mg
Sodium: 117 mg

Easy Coffee Cake with Walnut & Cinnamon Topping

Coffee Cake
3/4 c. sugar
3 T. butter, melted
2 eggs
1 1/2 c. milk
2 c. all-purpose flour
3 t. baking powder

1/4 t. salt
nonfat cooking spray

Walnut & Cinnamon Topping
3 T. sugar
3 t. ground cinnamon
1/2 c. walnuts, chopped

NUTRITIONAL ANALYSIS:
Calories: 339
Total fat: 12 g
Saturated fat: 4 g
% calories from fat: 31
Carbohydrates: 51 g
Protein: 8 g
Cholesterol: 71 mg
Sodium: 306 mg

*12 quart Contact Roaster: Spray the Baking Pan with the cooking spray. In a large mixing bowl, cream the sugar and butter. In a small bowl, whisk together the eggs and milk. Stir the milk into the butter. In a separate bowl, stir together the flour, baking powder and the salt. Add the dry ingredients into the creamed butter just until the flour is moistened. Spoon the batter into the Baking Pan. In a small bowl, combine the sugar, cinnamon and walnuts. Sprinkle over the top of the cake batter. Insert the Baking Pan into the Contact Roaster. Close the Lid and set the Timer for 45 to 55 minutes. A toothpick inserted in the cake will come out clean when the cake is done. Using oven mitts, remove the Baking Pan from the Contact Roaster and cool on a wire rack. Serves 8.

*4 quart Contact Roaster: Decrease the ingredients by one-third. Bake for 30 minutes and test the cake with a toothpick as directed above. Serves 4.

28

A "Lighter" Chocolate Cake

2 c. all-purpose flour
1 c. sugar
3/4 c. unsweetened cocoa
1/4 c. + 2 T.   cornstarch
3/4 t. baking soda
3/4 t. salt

1 1/2 t. vanilla extract
3/4 c. egg substitute
1 1/2 c. water
3/4 c. light or dark corn syrup
powdered sugar for dusting
nonfat cooking spray

*12 quart Contact Roaster: Preheat the Contact Roaster. Spray the Baking Pan with the cooking spray. In a large bowl, combine the flour, sugar, cocoa, cornstarch, baking soda and the salt until thoroughly mixed. In a medium bowl, whisk the vanilla, egg substitute, water and the corn syrup to blend. Stir the egg mixture into the dry ingredients until smooth. Pour the batter into the Baking Pan. Using oven mitts, place the Baking Pan into the Contact Roaster. Close the Lid and set the Timer for 45 to 50 minutes. The cake will be done when a toothpick inserted in the center comes out clean. Using oven mitts, remove the Baking Pan from the Contact Roaster and cool on a wire rack. Dust the top of the cake with the powdered sugar. Serves 10.

*4 quart Contact Roaster: Decrease the ingredients by one-third. Bake for 30 to 40 minutes and test the cake for doneness as directed above. Serves 4.

NUTRITIONAL ANALYSIS:

Calories: 288
Total fat: 1 g
Saturated fat: 1 g
% calories from fat: 3
Carbohydrates: 68 g
Protein: 6 g
Cholesterol: 0 mg
Sodium: 332 mg

Great Roast Beef, Pork & Lamb

When it comes to great beef, pork and lamb, there is no easier way to prepare excellent roasts, tenderloin and other large cuts of meat than in the George Foreman® Lean Mean Contact Roasting Machine.

Your Contact Roaster offers a more healthful way of preparing beef, pork and lamb by allowing the fat to drip away during the roasting process.

Because the Contact Roaster is compact and cooks using moisture, the juicy tenderness of meat is locked in, while the fat is quickly removed.

For a special occasion, try *Beef Ribeye Roast with Tarragon Red Bliss Potatoes, Flank Steak Rolled with Gorgonzola, Walnuts & Parsley* or *Fresh Peach & Pecan Stuffed Pork Chops.* Each of these entrées will bring a special satisfaction to your meal!

Garlic-Rubbed Cross Rib Roast

5 to 7 lbs. beef cross rib roast
4 cloves garlic, thinly sliced
1 clove garlic, peeled

1 1/2 t. salt
1 t. freshly ground black pepper

*12 quart Contact Roaster: Invert the Wire Rack and place it in the Contact Roaster. Preheat the Contact Roaster. Cut very thin, shallow slices over the entire surface of the roast and slip one piece of garlic inside each pocket. Rub the entire surface of the roast with the whole garlic clove and discard the clove. Salt and pepper the entire surface of the roast. Using oven mitts and a plastic or wooden utensil, place the roast on the Wire Rack in the Contact Roaster. Set the Timer to 130 to 160 minutes. Check for doneness and continue roasting, if desired. An internal meat thermometer should register at least 145°F for rare beef.

When done, place the roast on a carving board and let stand for 15 minutes. Carve into thin slices. Serves 12 to 16.

*4 quart Contact Roaster: Select a 3 to 4 pound roast and decrease the remaining ingredients by one-third. Place the roast directly on the bottom of the Contact Roaster and cook for 75 to 90 minutes, or until a meat thermometer registers at least 145°F for rare beef. Carve and serve as directed. Serves 6 to 8.

NUTRITIONAL ANALYSIS:

Calories: 378
Total fat: 29 g
Saturated fat: 12 g
% calories from fat: 71
Carbohydrates: <1 g
Protein: 27 g
Cholesterol: 94 mg
Sodium: 295 mg

Beef Ribeye Roast with Tarragon Red Bliss Potatoes

5 to 6 lbs. beef ribeye roast
3 lbs. baby red bliss potatoes, scrubbed and
    cut in half
1/4 c. extra virgin olive oil

1 t. salt
1 t. freshly ground black pepper
1/4 c. fresh tarragon, chopped

NUTRITIONAL ANALYSIS:

Calories: 428

Total fat: 31 g

Saturated fat: 12 g

% calories from fat: 67

Carbohydrates: 5 g

Protein: 30 g

Cholesterol: 100 mg

Sodium: 248 mg

*12 quart Contact Roaster: Invert the Wire Rack and place it in the Contact Roaster. Preheat the Contact Roaster. Place the cut potatoes in a large bowl. Whisk together the oil, salt, black pepper and tarragon and pour over the potatoes. Toss well to mix. Using oven mitts and a plastic or wooden spoon, place the beef roast on the Wire Rack. Use a long-handled plastic spoon to arrange the potatoes around the roast. Place the drip tray under the Contact Roaster and check it frequently while cooking. Set the Timer to 130 to 160 minutes. Check for doneness and continue roasting, if desired. An internal meat thermometer should register at least 145°F for rare beef. When done, place the roast on a carving board and let stand for 15 minutes. Carve into thin slices. Remove the potatoes from the Contact Roaster and arrange around the beef slices. Serves 12 to 15.

*4 quart Contact Roaster: Prepare a 3 to 4 pound roast and decrease the remaining ingredients by half. Set the Timer for 75 minutes for rare beef. Check for doneness as directed above. Serves 4 to 6.

San Antonio Beef Tenderloin

1 c. yellow onion, chopped
1 t. black pepper
1 c. celery, chopped
1 c. red bell pepper, chopped
1/2 c. green bell pepper, chopped
2 cloves garlic, minced
1 t. dry mustard

1 t. ground cumin
2 T. extra virgin olive oil
1/2 t. cayenne pepper
1/2 t. salt
1 t. black pepper
2 to 3 lb. beef tenderloin

*12 quart Contact Roaster: Invert the Wire Rack and place it in the Contact Roaster. Preheat the Contact Roaster. In a small bowl, mix together all of the ingredients except the beef tenderloin. Make cuts ½-inch in depth over the entire tenderloin and pat the vegetables and seasonings over the tenderloin to form a crust, pressing lightly.

Using oven mitts and a plastic or wooden utensil, place the roast on the Wire Rack in the Contact Roaster. Set the Timer for 60 to 90 minutes. An internal meat thermometer should read at least 145°F for rare beef. Remove the beef from the Contact Roaster and let stand for 15 minutes prior to serving. Carve in 1-inch slices and serve immediately. Serves 4 to 6.

*4 quart Contact Roaster: As directed above.

NUTRITIONAL ANALYSIS:
Calories: 364
Total fat: 29 g
Saturated fat: 11 g
% calories from fat: 71
Carbohydrates: 5 g
Protein: 21 g
Cholesterol: 79 mg
Sodium: 216 mg

50 Great George Foreman® Lean Mean Contact Roasting Machine Recipes!

33

Italian Ribeye Roast with Roasted Red Pepper & Pignolia Sauce

5 to 6 lbs. ribeye roast
1 t. salt
1 t. black pepper
1/2 t. garlic salt
1 c. roasted red peppers
1/4 c. extra virgin olive oil

3 T. pignolia nuts, lightly pan-toasted
1 1/2 T. balsamic vinegar
1 t. dried basil
1 clove garlic, crushed
1/2 t. salt
pinch ground allspice

*12 quart Contact Roaster: Preheat the Contact Roaster. Place the roast on the inverted Wire Rack in the Contact Roaster. Sprinkle the roast with salt, pepper and garlic salt. Set the Timer for 130 to 160 minutes. Check for doneness and continue roasting, if desired. An internal meat thermometer should register at least 145°F for rare beef. When done, let the roast stand for 15 minutes.

While the roast is standing, in a blender combine the roasted red peppers, olive oil, nuts, balsamic vinegar, basil, garlic, salt and allspice, and process on high speed until very smooth. Heat the sauce in a small saucepan until warm, but do not boil. To serve, drizzle a small amount of sauce over the sliced roast. Serves 15.

*4 quart Contact Roaster: Prepare a 3 to 4 pound roast and decrease the remaining ingredients by half. Set the Timer for 75 to 85 minutes for rare beef. Check for doneness as directed above. Serves 4 to 6.

Sirloin Steak Platter with Roasted Sweet Onions

2 1/2 lbs. sirloin steak, visible fat removed
1 t. salt
1 t. fresh oregano, minced
1 t. black pepper
1/4 c. cider vinegar

1/4 c. vegetable oil
2 T. prepared grainy Dijon mustard
2 cloves garlic, minced
4 sweet onions (such as Maui or Walla Walla),
    peeled and sliced 1/4-inch thick

*12 quart Contact Roaster: Place the steak in a large sealable plastic bag. Whisk together and add the salt, oregano, pepper, vinegar, oil, mustard and garlic. Combine the marinade in the bag thoroughly with the steak. Refrigerate for 6 to 12 hours.

Preheat the Contact Roaster. Using tongs, remove the steaks from the marinade. Discard the marinade. Using oven mitts and a plastic spatula, place the steaks in the Contact Roaster and add the sliced onions over and around the steaks. Set the Timer for 30 to 45 minutes. Roast the steaks until an internal meat thermometer registers at least 145°F for rare. Continue cooking, if desired, until done to your preference. Remove the steaks and onions from the Contact Roaster, slice into individual portions and serve while hot. Serves 6 to 8.

*4 quart Contact Roaster: Select a 1 to 1½ pound sirloin steak and decrease the remaining ingredients by half. Roast for 20 to 30 minutes and test with a meat thermometer as directed above. Serves 3 to 4.

NUTRITIONAL ANALYSIS:
Calories: 400
Total fat: 27 g
Saturated fat: 9 g
% calories from fat: 63
Carbohydrates: 7 g
Protein: 28 g
Cholesterol: 94 mg
Sodium: 460 mg

Flank Steak Rolled with Gorgonzola, Walnuts & Parsley

1 to 2 lbs. flank steak
1 c. prepared steak marinade

Gorgonzola Stuffing
1 1/2 c. soft bread crumbs

1 c. gorgonzola cheese, crumbled
1/2 c. walnuts, finely chopped
1/4 c. white onions, minced
1/4 c. fresh parsley, chopped
1 t. garlic, minced

*12 quart Contact Roaster: Mix together the bread crumbs, cheese, walnuts, onions, parsley and garlic. Place the steak on a flat working surface and discard the marinade. Shape the stuffing mixture down the middle third of the steak lengthwise and fold the 2 sides over the middle. Use cooking string to tie the rolled steak as tightly as possible.

Preheat the Contact Roaster. Using oven mitts and a wooden or plastic spatula, place the flank steak on the Wire Rack in the Contact Roaster. Set the Timer for 70 to 80 minutes. An internal meat thermometer will register 145°F for rare beef. Cook longer if desired. Remove the steak from the Contact Roaster and let stand for 10 minutes. Slice into pieces 1-inch thick. Serves 6 to 8.

*4 quart Contact Roaster: Cook for 60 to 70 minutes as directed above and test for doneness. Cook longer according to your preference.

Beef Tenderloin with Bleu Cheese au Jus

3 lbs. beef tenderloin, tied
2 t. butter or margarine
1 t. freshly ground black pepper
3 cloves garlic, minced

Blue Cheese Au Jus
1 T. lowfat butter

4 oz. bleu cheese, crumbled
2 c. beef broth
2 c. crimini mushrooms, cleaned and sliced
1/4 c. pecans, chopped
1/4 c. pine nuts, chopped
1/2 c. green onions, sliced

*12 quart Contact Roaster: Preheat the Contact Roaster. Cover the beef with the butter, sprinkle with salt and pepper and press the garlic into the beef surface. Using oven mitts and a wooden utensil, place the beef tenderloin on the inverted Wire Rack in the Contact Roaster. Set the Timer for 60 to 80 minutes. Check the beef when done. A meat thermometer will register 145ºF for rare beef. Cook longer if desired. Remove the beef from the Contact Roaster and let stand for 10 minutes. Whisk together the butter, cheese and broth in a saucepan. Heat to a simmer and add the mushrooms, pecans, pine nuts and onions. To serve, slice the beef and pour the sauce over all. Serves 8 to 10.

*4 quart Contact Roaster: Select a 1 to 1½ pound tenderloin. Decrease the remaining ingredients by half. Cook for 50 to 60 minutes and test as directed above. Serves 8 to 10.

NUTRITIONAL ANALYSIS:

Calories: 495
Total fat: 40 g
Saturated fat: 16 g
% calories from fat: 73
Carbohydrates: 3 g
Protein: 30 g
Cholesterol: 108 mg
Sodium: 405 mg

Sage & Cracked Pepper Pork Roast

4 to 5 lbs. pork center loin roast
2 T. extra virgin olive oil
1/4 c. fresh sage leaves, crumbled

1 t. salt
1 t. freshly cracked black pepper

NUTRITIONAL ANALYSIS:

Calories: 376
Total fat: 24 g
Saturated fat: 8 g
% calories from fat: 59
Carbohydrates: 1 g
Protein: 37 g
Cholesterol: 107 mg
Sodium: 311 mg

***12** quart Contact Roaster: Preheat the Contact Roaster. Place the pork roast on a flat working surface and cover with the olive oil. Sprinkle evenly with the sage, salt and pepper, pressing lightly to adhere the seasonings to the roast.

Using oven mitts and a wooden or plastic spatula, place the roast on the inverted Wire Rack in the Contact Roaster. Set the Timer for 160 to 180 minutes. An internal meat thermometer should register 160° to 170°F to properly cook the roast to medium. Cook longer according to your preference, if desired. Remove the roast from the Contact Roaster and let stand for 10 minutes. Slice evenly into pieces ½–inch thick. Serves 8 to 10.

***4** quart Contact Roaster: Select a 2 to 2½ pound pork roast. Decrease the remaining ingredients by one-half and cook for 70 to 80 minutes as directed above.

Spicy Thai Pork Roast

4 to 5 lbs. boneless pork roast
1 c. prepared catsup
2 t. chili powder
2 cloves garlic, minced

2 T. cider vinegar
1/2 t. salt
1 t. freshly ground black pepper

*12 quart Contact Roaster: Preheat the Contact Roaster. Place the roast on a flat working surface. Whisk together in a small bowl the catsup, chili powder, garlic, vinegar, salt and pepper. Using oven mitts and a plastic or wooden utensil, place the roast in the Contact Roaster. Brush the top and sides of the roast with the spicy sauce. Set the Timer for 60 minutes.

Carefully brush the top and sides of the roast again. Reset the Timer for 50 to 70 minutes. The roast is done when a meat thermometer reaches 160° to 170°F. Remove the roast from the Contact Roaster and let it stand for 10 minutes before slicing. Serves 10 to 12.

*4 quart Contact Roaster: Select a 3 pound roast and decrease the remaining ingredients by half. Cook for 70 to 80 minutes and test for doneness as directed above. Serves 6 to 8.

NUTRITIONAL ANALYSIS:
Calories: 312
Total fat: 18 g
Saturated fat: 6 g
% calories from fat: 52
Carbohydrates: 6 g
Protein: 31 g
Cholesterol: 89 mg
Sodium: 420 mg

Fresh Peach & Pecan Stuffed Pork Chops

6 double rib pork chops, each 2-inches thick
1/2 c. lowfat margarine
1/2 c. purple onions, minced
1/4 c. pecans, finely minced

1/2 c. fresh peaches, pitted, peeled and chopped
1 c. water
8 oz. herb-seasoned stuffing

NUTRITIONAL ANALYSIS:
Calories: 490
Total fat: 28 g
Saturated fat: 7 g
% calories from fat: 51
Carbohydrates: 31 g
Protein: 29 g
Cholesterol: 74 mg
Sodium: 797 mg

*12 quart Contact Roaster: Make a horizontal slice through the side of each chop to form a "pocket." Preheat the Contact Roaster. Toss together thoroughly the margarine, onions, pecans, peaches, water and herb stuffing. Spoon the stuffing into each pork chop pocket, packing lightly to fill. Place the chops in the Baking Pan.

Using oven mitts, place the Baking Pan in the Contact Roaster and cook for 110 to 130 minutes, or until a meat thermometer inserted in the center of a pork chop reads 160° to 170°F. Continue cooking, if desired, for your preference. Remove the chops from the Contact Roaster and serve while hot. Serves 6.

*4 quart Contact Roaster: Select 3 to 4 pork chops and decrease the remaining ingredients by half. Cook for 60 to 70 minutes as directed above.

Jalapeño Chile Mustard Pork Tenderloin

2 lbs. pork tenderloin
2 c. grainy Dijon mustard

2 jalapeño chilies, seeded and minced

*12 quart Contact Roaster: Place the pork tenderloin on the inverted Wire Rack in the Contact Roaster. Spoon the Dijon mustard over the top of the pork and sprinkle with the chilies. Set the Timer for 60 to 75 minutes.

An internal meat thermometer should register 160° to 170°F to properly cook the tenderloin to medium. Cook longer according to your preference, if desired. Remove the pork from the Contact Roaster and let stand for 10 minutes. Slice evenly into pieces ½-inch thick. Serves 6.

*4 quart Contact Roaster: Select a 1 to 1½ pound tenderloin. Decrease the mustard to 1 cup and use only 1 chile. Cook for 45 to 60 minutes and test for doneness as directed above.

NUTRITIONAL ANALYSIS:

Calories: 227
Total fat: 6 g
Saturated fat: 2 g
% calories from fat: 37
Carbohydrates: <1 g
Protein: 23 g
Cholesterol: 75 mg
Sodium: 1567 mg

Butterflied Pork Tenderloin with Cranberry Sauce

2 lbs. pork tenderloin
4 cloves garlic, minced
1/4 c. sweet onions, thinly sliced
2 t. fresh rosemary, minced
1 c. chicken broth

1 T. lemon zest
1 c. fresh cranberries, chopped (you may substitute frozen, thawed cranberries, if desired)
1/2 c. fresh orange juice
salt and black pepper to taste

NUTRITIONAL ANALYSIS:
Calories: 176
Total fat: 6 g
Saturated fat: 2 g
% calories from fat: 34
Carbohydrates: 5 g
Protein: 24 g
Cholesterol: 75 mg
Sodium: 201mg

*12 quart Contact Roaster: Preheat the Contact Roaster. Butterfly the pork by cutting it down the center lengthwise. Sprinkle the garlic over the tenderloin and wrap the tenderloin with cooking string to roll it securely. Using oven mitts and a wooden or plastic utensil, place the tenderloin in the Contact Roaster. Set the Timer for 60 to 75 minutes.

An internal meat thermometer should register 160° to 170°F to properly cook the tenderloin to medium. Remove the pork from the Contact Roaster and let stand for 10 minutes. Prepare the cranberry sauce by combining the onions, rosemary, broth, cranberries, lemon zest, orange juice and salt and pepper to taste.

Heat the sauce over low heat, stirring often, for 10 to 15 minutes. Slice the tenderloin into thin slices and pour the sauce over all. Serves 8.

*4 quart Contact Roaster: Select a 1 pound tenderloin and decrease the remaining ingredients by half. Cook for 45 to 60 minutes and test for doneness as directed above.

Cumin & Coriander Leg of Lamb

4 to 5 lbs. leg of lamb, semi-boneless (ask
   your butcher to remove as much of the
   bone as possible without butterflying
   the lamb)
1 T. extra virgin olive oil

2 T. ground coriander
2 T. ground cumin
1 T. freshly ground black pepper
2 t. sea salt

*12 quart Contact Roaster: Preheat the Contact Roaster. Place the lamb on a working surface and cover evenly with the olive oil. Sprinkle and press into the surface of the lamb the coriander, cumin, pepper and salt.

Using oven mitts and a wooden or plastic utensil, place the lamb on the inverted Wire Rack in the Contact Roaster. Set the Timer for 130 to 175 minutes. When ready, a meat ther-mometer should read at least 150ºF for rare. Cook longer, if desired. Remove from the Contact Roaster and let stand for 10 minutes prior to carving. Serves 10.

*4 quart Contact Roaster: Select a 3 pound leg of lamb and decrease the remaining ingredients by half. Cook for 80 minutes and test for doneness as directed above. Serves 4 to 5.

NUTRITIONAL ANALYSIS:
Calories: 482
Total fat: 38 g
Saturated fat: 18 g
% calories from fat: 72
Carbohydrates: 1 g
Protein: 32 g
Cholesterol: 120 mg
Sodium: 582 mg

Boneless Ham with Apricot Glaze

1/2 c. dark brown sugar, packed
1 T. cornstarch
1/2 t. fresh gingerroot, grated
1/4 t. salt

12 oz. apricot nectar
1 T. lemon juice
4 to 6 lbs. boneless ham, fully cooked

NUTRITIONAL
ANALYSIS:
Calories: 208
Total fat: 9 g
Saturated fat: 2 g
% calories from fat: 38
Carbohydrates: 10 g
Protein: 21 g
Cholesterol: 83 mg
Sodium: 1347 mg

*12 quart Contact Roaster: Combine in a small saucepan, the sugar, cornstarch, gingerroot and salt. Heat and stir over medium heat until the sugar dissolves. Slowly add the apricot nectar and heat until the sauce simmers and is thickened. Add the lemon juice and stir again. Remove from the heat and set aside.

Preheat the Contact Roaster. Using oven mitts and a wooden or plastic utensil, place the ham on the inverted Wire Rack in the Contact Roaster and brush heavily with the glaze. Set the Timer for 60 minutes. Brush the ham again with the glaze and reset the Timer for 30 minutes. The ham is done when it is hot throughout. Remove the ham and carve into thin slices. Serves 16.

*4 quart Contact Roaster: Select a 2 to 3 pound ham. Prepare the sauce and cook for 45 to 60 minutes as directed above. Serves 8 to 10.

50 Great George Foreman® Lean Mean Contact Roasting Machine Recipes!

Greek Roasted Lamb with Rosemary Potatoes

3 T. extra virgin olive oil
5 large Russet potatoes, scrubbed, unpeeled and
    roughly cut into eighths
1 t. salt
1 t. freshly ground black pepper

2 T. extra virgin olive oil
5 to 6 lbs. bone-in leg of lamb, visible fat removed
1/4 c. fresh rosemary, finely minced, divided
5 cloves garlic, minced
1 t. freshly ground black pepper

*12 quart Contact Roaster: Preheat the Contact Roaster. In a large bowl, combine the oil, potatoes, salt and pepper. Set aside. Using oven mitts and a plastic or wooden utensil, place the leg of lamb on the inverted Wire Rack in the Contact Roaster. Sprinkle the lamb with the olive oil, half of the rosemary, garlic and pepper. Set the Timer for 60 minutes.

Carefully open the Contact Roaster and add the potatoes around the lamb. Sprinkle with the remaining rosemary. Reset the Timer for 70 to 100 minutes. Test the lamb for doneness by inserting a meat thermometer into the thickest part of the meat. The thermometer should register at least 150°F for rare. When done, remove the lamb and potatoes from the Contact Roaster. Allow the lamb to stand for 10 minutes before carving. Serve with the roasted potatoes. Serves 10 to 12.

*4 quart Contact Roaster: Select a 3 to 4 pound leg of lamb and decrease the remaining ingredients by one-third. Roast for 70 to 80 minutes and test for doneness as directed above.

NUTRITIONAL ANALYSIS:

Calories: 470
Total fat: 36 g
Saturated fat: 14 g
% calories from fat: 70
Carbohydrates: 7 g
Protein: 29 g
Cholesterol: 107 mg
Sodium: 249 mg

CHAPTER 5

Great Roast Chicken, Turkey & Seafood

One of the outstanding features of your George Foreman® Lean Mean Contact Roasting Machine is the effortless way in which you can prepare poultry. A roasted whole chicken or turkey may seem like an entrée that requires special, detailed preparation, however, with your Contact Roaster, you will find that roasting chicken, turkey, duck and other game birds is a quick and easy process. Invite your family to dinner and serve *Chinese Five-Spice Chicken, Herbes de Provence Roasted* *Chicken* or *Jamaican Jerked Chicken.* Each of these entrées requires only a light salad and steamed vegetables to complete a satisfying, yet nutritious meal.

In addition to the poultry recipes in this chapter, you'll find recipes for seafood and fish that invite healthful eating patterns. Consider *Hawaiian Mahi-Mahi with Mango-Pineapple Salsa* and *Spinach Florentine Fillet of Sole.* Each of these entrées provides good–for–you fish and fruit or vegetables that have been baked or poached with little or no fat.

Lemon Thyme Roasted Chicken

3 to 4 lbs. whole chicken, cleaned and
    giblets removed
2 T. extra virgin olive oil
1 t. salt
1 t. black pepper

juice one lemon
1 T. fresh thyme, minced
1 T. fresh tarragon, minced
1 T. fresh parsley, minced

*12 quart Contact Roaster: Preheat the Contact Roaster. Place the chicken on a flat working surface and brush the oil over the chicken evenly. Sprinkle the salt and pepper over the oil. Using oven mitts and a plastic or wooden utensil, place the chicken in the Contact Roaster and sprinkle with the lemon juice. Lightly cover with the herbs. Cover and set the Timer for 60 to 75 minutes. The chicken will be done when a meat thermometer inserted into the thickest part of the meat registers 180°F. Allow the chicken to stand for 10 minutes before carving. Remove the skin before eating. Serves 4 to 5.

*4 quart Contact Roaster: Select a 3 to 4 pound chicken and roast for 60 minutes as directed above. Serves 3 to 4.

NUTRITIONAL ANALYSIS:
Calories: 462
Total fat: 15 g
Saturated fat: 3g
% calories from fat: 31
Carbohydrates: 2 g
Protein: 74 g
Cholesterol: 236 mg
Sodium: 738 mg

Chinese Five-Spice Chicken

4 to 5 lbs. whole chicken, cleaned and
    giblets removed
2 cloves garlic, minced

2 thin slices fresh ginger
2 T. sesame oil
1 T. Chinese five-spice powder

*12 quart Contact Roaster: Preheat the Contact Roaster. Place the chicken on a flat working surface. Rub the garlic over the chicken and discard the garlic. Rub the ginger slices over the chicken and discard the ginger. Lightly brush the sesame oil over the chicken and dust the chicken with the five–spice powder.

Using oven mitts and a plastic or wooden utensil, place the chicken in the Contact Roaster.

Cover and set the Timer for 60 to 75 minutes. The chicken will be done when a meat thermometer inserted into the thickest part of the meat registers at least 180°F. Allow the chicken to stand for 10 minutes before carving. Remove the skin before eating. Serves 6.

*4 quart Contact Roaster: Select a 3 to 4 pound chicken and roast for 60 minutes as directed above. Serves 3 to 4.

NUTRITIONAL ANALYSIS:

Calories: 459
Total fat: 16 g
Saturated fat: 2 g
% calories from fat: 32
Carbohydrates: 2 g
Protein: 74 g
Cholesterol: 236 mg
Sodium: 274 mg

Roasted Chicken with Summer Vegetables

4 to 5 lbs. whole chicken, cleaned and
    giblets removed
1/2 c. lowfat margarine
1 T. rosemary, crushed
1 t. salt
1/2 t. black pepper

1 clove garlic, minced
6 new red potatoes, cleaned and cut in half
6 carrots, cleaned and cut in half crosswise
2 white onions, peeled and cut into quarters
2 T. fresh parsley, chopped

*12 quart Contact Roaster: Preheat the Contact Roaster. Place the chicken on a flat working surface. Mix together in a small bowl, the margarine, rosemary, salt, pepper and garlic. Pat the herb butter over the chicken.

Using oven mitts and a plastic or wooden utensil, place the chicken in the Contact Roaster. Arrange the potatoes, carrots and onions around the chicken in the Contact Roaster. Cover and set the Timer for 60 to 75 minutes.

The chicken will be done when a meat thermometer inserted into the thickest part of the meat registers at least 180°F. Use a slotted plastic spoon to remove the vegetables and arrange on a platter. Allow the chicken to stand for 10 minutes before carving. Remove the skin before eating. Serves 6.

*4 quart Contact Roaster: Select a 3 to 4 pound chicken and roast for 60 minutes as directed above. Serves 3 to 4.

NUTRITIONAL ANALYSIS:
Calories: 456
Total fat: 12 g
Saturated fat: 3 g
% calories from fat: 25
Carbohydrates: 19 g
Protein: 66 g
Cholesterol: 197 mg
Sodium: 796 mg

Herbes de Provence Roasted Chicken

4 to 5 lbs. whole chicken, cleaned and
    giblets removed
1/4 c. extra virgin olive oil
1/4 c. cider vinegar
1/2 c. water

2 T. herbes de Provence
2 T. lemon juice
1 t. salt
1 t. black pepper
2 T. fresh parsley, chopped

*12 quart Contact Roaster: Place the chicken in a large self-sealing plastic bag. Whisk together the oil, vinegar, water, herbes de Provence, lemon juice, salt and pepper and pour over the chicken. Mix the marinade thoroughly with the chicken. Seal the plastic bag and refrigerate the chicken for 1 to 4 hours, turning the chicken occasionally.

Preheat the Contact Roaster. Discard the marinade. Using oven mitts and a plastic or wooden utensil, place the chicken in the Contact Roaster. Cover and set the Timer for 60 to 75 minutes. The chicken will be done when a meat thermometer inserted into the thickest part of the meat registers at least 180°F. Allow the chicken to stand for 10 minutes before carving. Garnish with the parsley. Remove the skin before eating. Serves 6.

*4 quart Contact Roaster: Select a 3 to 4 pound chicken and roast for 60 minutes as directed above. Serves 3 to 4.

NUTRITIONAL ANALYSIS:
Calories: 510
Total fat: 21 g
Saturated fat: 4 g
% calories from fat: 39
Carbohydrates: 2 g
Protein: 74 g
Cholesterol: 236 mg
Sodium: 1123 mg

Dijon Mustard & Lemon Chicken

4 to 5 lbs. whole chicken, cleaned and
    giblets removed
1/2 c. rice vinegar
1/2 c. water

1/4 c. prepared Dijon mustard
2 T. lemon juice
1 t. black pepper

*12 quart Contact Roaster: Place the chicken in a large self-sealing plastic bag. Whisk together the vinegar, water, Dijon mustard, lemon juice and pepper and pour over the chicken. Mix the marinade thoroughly with the chicken. Seal the plastic bag and refrigerate the chicken for 1 to 4 hours, turning the chicken occasionally.

Preheat the Contact Roaster. Discard the marinade. Using oven mitts and a plastic or wooden utensil, place the chicken in the Contact Roaster. Cover and set the Timer for 60 to 75 minutes. The chicken will be done when a meat thermometer inserted into the thickest part of the meat registers at least 180°F. Allow the chicken to stand for 10 minutes before carving. Remove the skin before eating. Serves 4 to 5.

*4 quart Contact Roaster: Select a 3 to 4 pound chicken and roast for 60 minutes as directed above. Serves 3 to 4.

NUTRITIONAL ANALYSIS:

Calories: 431
Total fat: 10 g
Saturated fat: 2 g
% calories from fat: 23
Carbohydrates: 1 g
Protein: 74 g
Cholesterol: 236 mg
Sodium: 562 mg

50 Great George Foreman® Lean Mean Contact Roasting Machine Recipes!

51

Orange Marmalade Cornish Hens

4 to 6 Cornish game hens, cleaned and
    giblets removed
4 lemons, quartered
4 shallots, chopped

1 c. orange marmalade
1/4 c. extra virgin olive oil
1 t. fresh marjoram, crushed

*12 quart Contact Roaster: Preheat the Contact Roaster. Place the game hens on a flat working surface. Lightly fill the cavities of each hen with the lemons and shallots. Mix together in a small bowl, the orange marmalade, olive oil and marjoram and whisk until smooth.

Using oven mitts and a plastic or wooden utensil, place the game hens on the inverted Wire Rack in the Contact Roaster. Brush with the orange marmalade glaze. Cover and set the Timer for 60 to 75 minutes. The hens will be done when a meat thermometer inserted into the thickest part of the meat registers at least 180°F. Use a slotted plastic spoon to remove the hens and arrange on a platter. Remove the skin before eating. Serves 4 to 6.

*4 quart Contact Roaster: Select 2 game hens and reduce the remaining ingredients by half. Roast for 60 minutes as directed above. Serves 2.

Jamaican Jerked Chicken

4 to 5 lbs. whole chicken, cleaned and
   giblets removed
1/4 c. vegetable oil
4 cloves garlic, minced
1 large purple onion, peeled and roughly
   chopped
2 habañero peppers, seeded and chopped

2 T. fresh parsley, chopped
1/4 c. cider vinegar
1/4 c. dark brown sugar, packed
1/4 t. ground cinnamon
1/8 t. ground cloves
1 1/2 t. ground allspice
1/4 c. fresh lime juice

*12 quart Contact Roaster: Place the chicken in a large self-sealing plastic bag. Place in a blender the remaining ingredients. Process at high speed until smooth. Pour the marinade over the chicken and mix thoroughly with the chicken. Seal the plastic bag and refrigerate the chicken for 2 to 6 hours, turning the chicken occasionally.

Preheat the Contact Roaster. Discard the marinade. Using oven mitts and a plastic or wooden utensil, place the chicken in the Contact Roaster. Cover and set the Timer to 60 to 75 minutes. The chicken will be done when a meat thermometer inserted into the thickest part of the meat registers at least 180°F. Allow the chicken to stand for 10 minutes before carving. Remove the skin before eating. Serves 6.

*4 quart Contact Roaster: Select a 3 to 4 pound chicken and roast for 60 minutes as directed above. Serves 3 to 4.

NUTRITIONAL ANALYSIS:

Calories: 472
Total fat: 17 g
Saturated fat: 3 g
% calories from fat: 34
Carbohydrates: 14 g
Protein: 62 g
Cholesterol: 197 mg
Sodium: 230 mg

Cornish Game Hens with Sage & Summer Squash

4 to 6 Cornish game hens, cleaned and dried
16 whole baby carrots
4 c. summer squash, cut into large chunks
10 baby red bliss potatoes, cleaned

3 cloves garlic, minced
1 1/2 t. salt
1 t. fresh sage, crumbled
1/2 t. freshly ground black pepper

NUTRITIONAL ANALYSIS:
Calories: 302
Total fat: 6 g
Saturated fat: 1 g
% calories from fat: 17
Carbohydrates: 24 g
Protein: 40 g
Cholesterol: 145 mg
Sodium: 722 mg

*12 quart Contact Roaster: Preheat the Contact Roaster. Using oven mitts and a plastic or wooden utensil, place the game hens on the inverted Wire Rack in the Contact Roaster. Arrange the carrots, squash, potatoes and garlic around the hens. Mix together the salt, sage and pepper and sprinkle over the hens and vegetables. Cover and set the Timer for 60 to 75 minutes. The hens will be done when a meat thermometer inserted into the thickest part of the meat registers at least 180°F. Use a slotted plastic spoon to remove the vegetables and hens and arrange on a platter. Remove the skin before eating. Serves 4 to 6.

*4 quart Contact Roaster: Select 2 game hens and reduce the remaining ingredients by half. Roast for 60 minutes as directed above. Serves 2.

Turkey Breast with Creamy Horseradish Sauce

1 T. prepared creamy horseradish
1/2 c. yellow onion, diced
1/2 c. catsup
1/4 c. Worcestershire sauce

1 T. sugar
1 t. dry mustard
3 to 4 lbs. boneless turkey breast, cleaned
and dried

*12 quart Contact Roaster: Mix together the creamy horseradish, onion, catsup, Worcestershire sauce, sugar and dry mustard. Set aside.

Preheat the Contact Roaster. Using oven mitts and a plastic or wooden utensil, place the turkey on the inverted Wire Rack in the Contact Roaster. Brush with one–half of the sauce. Cover and set the Timer for 60 minutes. Open the Contact Roaster and brush the turkey with the remaining sauce. Set the Timer for 30 to 40 minutes. The turkey will be done when a meat thermometer inserted into the thickest part of the meat registers at least 180°F. Allow the turkey to stand for 10 minutes before carving. Serves 6.

*4 quart Contact Roaster: Select a 1½ to 2 pound turkey or capon breast and roast for a total of 60 minutes, checking for doneness as directed above. Serves 3 to 4.

NUTRITIONAL ANALYSIS:
Calories: 196
Total fat: 4 g
Saturated fat: <1 g
% calories from fat: 10
Carbohydrates: 11 g
Protein: 58 g
Cholesterol: 141 mg
Sodium: 452 mg

50 Great George Foreman® Lean Mean Contact Roasting Machine Recipes!

55

Fresh Ginger & Orange Marinated Turkey Breast

3 to 4 lbs. boneless turkey breast, cleaned
  and dried
1 c. fresh orange juice
1/4 c. light molasses

1 T. fresh gingerroot, finely grated
4 cloves garlic, minced
1/4 c. vegetable oil

*12 quart Contact Roaster: Place the turkey breast in a large self-sealing plastic bag. Mix together the orange juice, molasses, gingerroot, garlic and vegetable oil and pour over the turkey. Seal the bag and refrigerate for 1 to 4 hours, turning the turkey occasionally.

Preheat the Contact Roaster. Using oven mitts and a plastic or wooden utensil, place the turkey on the inverted Wire Rack in the Contact Roaster. Discard the marinade. Cover and set the Timer for 80 to 100 minutes. The turkey will be done when a meat thermometer inserted into the thickest part of the meat registers at least 180°F. Allow the turkey to stand for 10 minutes before carving. Serves 6.

*4 quart Contact Roaster: Select a 1½ to 2 pound turkey or capon breast and roast for a total of 60 minutes, checking for doneness as directed above. Serves 3 to 4.

NUTRITIONAL ANALYSIS:
Calories: 392
Total fat: 11 g
Saturated fat: 2 g
% calories from fat: 25
Carbohydrates: 15 g
Protein: 56 g
Cholesterol: 141 mg
Sodium: 117 mg

Homestyle Roasted Turkey

10 to 12 lbs. whole turkey, cleaned and dried
2 t. salt
2 t. black pepper
2 T. extra virgin olive oil

3 lemons, cut into quarters
1 lime, cut into quarters
2 white onions, peeled and cut into quarters

*12 quart Contact Roaster: Place the turkey on a flat working surface. Mix together the salt, pepper and oil and cover the entire turkey with the spice mixture. Preheat the Contact Roaster.

Using oven mitts and a plastic or wooden utensil, place the turkey on the inverted Wire Rack in the Contact Roaster. Set the Timer for 130 to 160 minutes. The turkey will be done when a meat thermometer inserted into the thickest part of the meat registers at least 180°F. Allow the turkey to stand for 20 minutes before carving. Remove the skin before eating. Serves 10 to 12.

NUTRITIONAL ANALYSIS:
Calories: 485
Total fat: 13 g
Saturated fat: 4 g
% calories from fat: 26
Carbohydrates: 4 g
Protein: 83 g
Cholesterol: 246 mg
Sodium: 653 mg

Tandoori Turkey Medallions

2 to 3 lbs. turkey tenderloins, cut into 12 to 14 pieces
2 c. plain nonfat yogurt
2 T. fresh ginger, finely grated
1 clove garlic, minced
2 T. vegetable oil

1 T. ground paprika
2 t. ground cumin
2 t. ground turmeric
1/4 t. cayenne pepper
1 t. salt
1/2 t. black pepper

NUTRITIONAL ANALYSIS:
Calories: 191
Total fat: 4 g
Saturated fat: 1 g
% calories from fat: 21
Carbohydrates: 6 g
Protein: 31 g
Cholesterol: 77 mg
Sodium: 389 mg

*12 quart Contact Roaster: Place the tenderloins in a shallow glass dish. In a medium plastic or glass bowl, combine the yogurt, ginger, garlic, vegetable oil, paprika, cumin, turmeric, cayenne pepper, salt and black pepper. Whisk together and pour over the turkey tenderloins. Cover the turkey with plastic wrap and refrigerate for 4 hours, turning the turkey every hour.

Preheat the Contact Roaster. Place the turkey in the Baking Pan and discard the marinade.

Using oven mitts, place the Baking Pan in the Contact Roaster and set the Timer for 50 to 70 minutes. The turkey medallions will be done when no pink remains and the turkey is hot throughout. Remove and serve while hot. Serves 6 to 8.

*4 quart Contact Roaster: Select 1 to 2 pounds of turkey tenderloin and decrease the remaining ingredients by half. Roast the turkey for 30 to 40 minutes as directed above. Serves 3 to 4.

Tropical Lime & Cilantro Chicken Breasts

6 boneless, skinless chicken breasts
2 c. pineapple juice
1/4 c. soy sauce
2 T. vegetable oil
1/4 c. honey

3 cloves garlic, minced
1 t. salt
1/2 t. freshly ground black pepper
1 T. fresh cilantro, chopped

*12 quart Contact Roaster: Place the chicken breasts in a shallow glass pan. Mix together the remaining ingredients and pour over the chicken. Cover the chicken with plastic wrap and refrigerate for 2 to 4 hours, turning the chicken occasionally.

Preheat the Contact Roaster. Place the chicken breasts in the Baking Pan and discard the marinade. Using oven mitts, place the Baking Pan in the Contact Roaster and set the Timer for 50 to 70 minutes. The chicken will be done when no pink remains and a meat thermometer registers 180°F. Remove and serve while hot. Serves 6.

*4 quart Contact Roaster: Select 4 chicken breasts and decrease the remaining ingredients by half. Roast the chicken for 30 to 40 minutes as directed above. Serves 4.

NUTRITIONAL ANALYSIS:

Calories: **205**
Total fat: **5 g**
Saturated fat: **1 g**
% calories from fat: **24**
Carbohydrates: **21 g**
Protein: **18 g**
Cholesterol: **41 mg**
Sodium: **1052 mg**

Hawaiian Mahi-Mahi with Mango-Pineapple Salsa

3 lbs. fresh mahi-mahi fillets
salt and white pepper to taste
2 c. fresh mangos, diced
2 c. fresh pineapple, diced
1/2 c. purple onion, minced

1/2 t. freshly ground black pepper
1 t. salt
2 T. fresh lime juice
fresh cilantro for garnish

NUTRITIONAL ANALYSIS:

Calories: 197
Total fat: 1 g
Saturated fat: <1 g
% calories from fat: 7
Carbohydrates: 13 g
Protein: 32 g
Cholesterol: 125 mg
Sodium: 462 mg

*12 quart Contact Roaster: Preheat the Contact Roaster. Place the fish fillets in the Baking Pan and salt and pepper to taste. Using oven mitts, place the Baking Pan in the Contact Roaster and set the Timer for 20 to 30 minutes, or until the fish flakes easily with a fork and is opaque throughout.

Prepare the salsa by combining the mangos, pineapple, onion, black pepper, salt and lime juice in a large serving bowl. Toss well and refrigerate. When the fish fillets are done, serve each with a spoonful of salsa over the top. Garnish each serving with cilantro. Serves 6 to 8.

*4 quart Contact Roaster: Select 1 to 1½ pounds of mahi mahi and decrease the remaining ingredients by half. Cook for 20 to 25 minutes as directed above. Serves 3 to 4.

50 Great George Foreman® Lean Mean Contact Roasting Machine Recipes!

Moroccan Salmon Steaks

2 lbs. salmon steaks, about 1-inch thick
1/4 c. extra virgin olive oil
1/4 c. water
1/4 c. fresh lemon juice
1/4 c. fresh parsley, minced
1/4 c. fresh cilantro, minced
1 T. fresh gingerroot, grated

1 t. ground cumin
1 clove garlic, minced
1 t. paprika
1/2 t. salt
1/4 t. cayenne pepper
1/4 t. black pepper

*12 quart Contact Roaster: Place the salmon steaks in a shallow glass pan. In a blender, combine the remaining ingredients. Process on high speed until very smooth. Pour the marinade over the salmon and turn once to coat the steaks. Cover tightly with plastic wrap and refrigerate the steaks for 1 to 4 hours.

Preheat the Contact Roaster. Place the steaks in the Baking Pan and discard the marinade.

Using oven mitts, place the Baking Pan in the Contact Roaster. Set the Timer for 30 minutes. The fish will be done when it flakes easily with a fork. Continue roasting for 10 minutes, if needed. Serves 4 to 6.

*4 quart Contact Roaster: Select 1 pound of salmon steaks and decrease the remaining ingredients by half. Roast for 20 to 30 minutes, or until the fish flakes easily with a fork.

NUTRITIONAL ANALYSIS:

Calories: 367
Total fat: 25 g
Saturated fat: 5 g
% calories from fat: 64
Carbohydrates: 2 g
Protein: 31 g
Cholesterol: 100 mg
Sodium: 268 mg

Spinach Florentine Fillet of Sole

4 large Petrale sole fillets
2 small tomatoes, cored and diced
1/2 c. white onion, diced
2 – 10 oz. pkgs. frozen chopped spinach,
   thawed and well-drained

2 t. salt
1 t. freshly ground black pepper
1/2 c. Parmesan cheese, grated

**NUTRITIONAL
ANALYSIS:**

Calories: 122
Total fat: 3 g
Saturated fat: 1 g
% calories from fat: 20
Carbohydrates: 4 g
Protein: 19 g
Cholesterol: 43 mg
Sodium: 840 mg

*12 quart Contact Roaster: Preheat the Contact Roaster. Place the fillets in the Baking Pan and spread the diced tomatoes over the top of the fillets. Scatter the onion over the tomatoes and layer the spinach over all. Add the salt and pepper and sprinkle the Parmesan cheese over the top.

Using oven mitts, place the Baking Pan in the Contact Roaster and set the Timer for 40 to 50 minutes. The fish is done when the fish is opaque and flakes easily with a fork. Serves 8.

*4 quart Contact Roaster: Select 2 large sole fillets and decrease the remaining ingredients by half. Roast for 20 to 30 minutes, check for doneness, and continue cooking if needed. Serves 4.

Index

RECIPES!

LEAN MEAN FAT REDUCING GRILLING MACHINE

GEORGE FOREMAN

80 GREAT

Pascoe Publishing, Inc.
Rocklin CA 95765

ISBN: 1-929862-33-4

03   04   05   06   10 9 8 7 6 5 4 3 2 1

All books are printed in China.

TABLE OF CONTENTS

CHAPTER 1

Introduction to Your George Foreman®
Lean Mean Fat Reducing Grilling Machine

George Foreman is a familiar face and a popular icon to millions of people around the world. A champion in his own right as the heavyweight boxing champion of the world, George Foreman also has earned worldwide recognition as the man behind the George Foreman® Lean Mean Fat Reducing Grilling Machine. This unique and remarkable grill has become the indoor/outdoor grill of choice for millions of people and the reason why is found within the patented construction of the grill–special grids channel away the fat from foods as they grill quickly and easily. Foods are grilled in just minutes, without added fat!

Within the pages of this cookbook, you'll find an array of recipes specifically created for the George Foreman® Lean Mean Fat Reducing Grilling

Machine. Look for exciting new ways to prepare burgers, sandwiches, steaks and chops. Grilling is so extremely easy that you'll often reach for your Grilling Machine instead of skillets, frying pans and other hard-to-clean cookware. The following hints will help you get the best results from your grilling and will maximize the life of your grill.

★ The plates of your Grilling Machine have a special nonstick coating that eliminates the need for additional butter or oil when grilling. To protect the nonstick coating, use only heat-resistant plastic utensils when placing food in or removing food from the grill. Metal utensils will scratch or mar the surface of the plates.

★ Your Grilling Machine grills quickly and efficiently, so foods will become quite hot when they are ready to serve. Use oven mitts to remove hot foods and open and close the Grilling Machine carefully. Do not allow young children to operate the Grilling Machine.

★ Follow the manufacturer's instructions carefully when using the Drip Trays. Foods that naturally contain fat, such as beef steaks, will produce fat and liquids that will flow into the Drip Tray. If the Drip Tray becomes full while grilling, use oven mitts to remove it carefully. Drain and reuse, if needed. If the Drip Tray does not require draining while grilling, let the Drip Tray stand until the fat and liquids have completely cooled before removing and draining.

★ Grill poultry with the skin on, if desired, but remove it before eating to greatly reduce the amount of fat consumed. Remove visible fat from beef, pork and lamb before grilling. Grill fish steaks with the skin on and remove the skin after grilling.

★ Find a permanent place on your kitchen counter for your George Foreman® Lean Mean Fat Reducing Grilling Machine. Once you've tried a few easy recipes in your Grilling Machine, you'll want to use it every day!

CHAPTER 2

Great Sandwiches, Burgers & Snacks

Your George Foreman® Lean Mean Fat Reducing Grilling Machine is made to perfectly grill all of your favorite snacks, sandwiches and burgers. Good snacks, sandwiches and burgers start with good ingredients, such as extra lean ground round beef, lean ground turkey, lean ground chicken and meatless patties for burgers. Lowfat smoked turkey, ham and chicken are excellent choices for sandwiches and snacks. Whole grain breads and rolls offer nutritional value and fiber and fresh vegetables and fruit can round out a satisfying meal.

You'll have no need to drive through the fast food lane anymore!

You may already have a favorite burger recipe for grilling and you'll find that your recipes work easily in the George Foreman® Lean Mean Fat Reducing Grilling Machine. Remember to handle the meat as little as possible to avoid overmixing and use fresh herbs and minced vegetables for added flavor. You do not need to add butter or oil to grill your burgers. Your burgers will be delightfully moist and tender!

The Classic Beef Burger

1 lb. extra lean ground round beef
1 T. Worcestershire sauce
1/2 t. ground black pepper
1 t. garlic salt

3 T. yellow onion, minced
4 large sesame seed hamburger buns
nonfat cooking spray

In a medium bowl, use your hands to toss lightly together the ground round, Worcestershire sauce, black pepper, garlic salt and yellow onion until the ingredients are evenly distributed. Shape the mixture into 4 hamburger patties. Lightly coat the grill with the cooking spray and preheat for 5 minutes. Place the hamburgers on the grill and cook for 7 to 8 minutes, depending on your preference. Lightly toast the buns under the oven broiler, if desired. Serve the grilled hamburgers and buns with condiments of your choice. Serves 4.

NUTRITIONAL ANALYSIS:

Calories: 384
Total fat: 22 g
Saturated fat: 8 g
% calories from fat: 50
Carbohydrates: 23 g
Protein: 25 g
Cholesterol: 78 mg
Sodium: 661 mg

Smokey BBQ Beef Burgers

2 T. Worcestershire sauce
2 T. bottled liquid smoke
1/2 c. tomato sauce
1 T. brown sugar
1 T. prepared mustard

1/2 t. seasoned salt
1/4 t. ground black pepper
1 lb. extra lean ground round beef
4 large hamburger buns
nonfat cooking spray

In a medium bowl, stir together the Worcestershire sauce, liquid smoke, tomato sauce, brown sugar, prepared mustard, salt and the black pepper. Add the beef and toss lightly without overmixing. Shape the mixture into 4 hamburger patties. Lightly spray the grill with the cooking spray and preheat for 5 minutes. Place the patties on the grill and cook for 7 to 8 minutes, depending on your preference. Lightly toast the buns under the oven broiler, if desired, and serve with the grilled hamburgers and condiments of your choice. Serves 4.

NUTRITIONAL ANALYSIS:
Calories: 405
Total fat: 23 g
Saturated fat: 8 g
% calories from fat: 48
Carbohydrates: 28 g
Protein: 26 g
Cholesterol: 78 mg
Sodium: 682 mg

Dijon Mustard Turkey Burgers

1 lb. lean ground turkey
3 T. Dijon mustard
2 T. nonfat mayonnaise
3 T. white onion, minced

1 t. seasoned salt
1 t. ground white pepper
4 whole wheat buns
nonfat cooking spray

In a medium bowl, mix together the ground turkey, Dijon mustard, mayonnaise, onion, seasoned salt and the white pepper until the ingredients are evenly distributed. Shape the mixture into 4 patties. Spray the grill with cooking spray and preheat for 5 minutes. Place the patties on the grill and cook for 7 to 8 minutes, depending on your preference. Toast the whole wheat buns under the broiler and serve with the grilled turkey burgers and condiments of your choice. Serves 4.

NUTRITIONAL ANALYSIS:

Calories: 305
Total fat: 12 g
Saturated fat: 3 g
% calories from fat: 37
Carbohydrates: 21 g
Protein: 24 g
Cholesterol: 90 mg
Sodium: 873 mg

"Some Like It Hot" Italian Sausage Burger

1 lb. uncooked Italian turkey sausage
1/4 c. fresh or prepared salsa
1 to 2 t. hot pepper sauce (optional)
1/4 t. ground black pepper
1 egg white

1/4 c. seasoned bread crumbs
6 large sourdough buns
nonfat cooking spray
1/3 c. Jack cheese, shredded

Remove the sausage from the casings and place the sausage in a medium bowl. Add to the sausage the salsa, hot pepper sauce, black pepper, egg white and the bread crumbs. Combine thoroughly, mixing with your hands. Shape the meat mixture into 4 patties. Spray the grill with cooking spray and preheat for 5 minutes. Place the patties on the grill and cook for 7 to 8 minutes, or until the burgers are no longer pink in the center. Toast the sourdough buns under the broiler. Place the patties on the toasted buns and sprinkle Jack cheese over each patty. Serves 6.

NUTRITIONAL ANALYSIS:

Calories: 332
Total fat: 24 g
Saturated fat: 8 g
% calories from fat: 41
Carbohydrates: 19 g
Protein: 15 g
Cholesterol: 46 mg
Sodium: 801 mg

Grilled Portobello Mushroom Sandwiches

2 portobello mushrooms, thickly sliced
2 T. extra virgin olive oil, divided
2 t. balsamic vinegar, divided
1/4 t. ground black pepper, divided
1/2 t. seasoned salt, divided

1/2 small red onion, thinly sliced
1 green bell pepper, thinly sliced
2 T. fresh Italian parsley chopped
4 onion rolls, split
nonfat cooking spray

NUTRITIONAL ANALYSIS:

Calories: 202
Total fat: 9 g
Saturated fat: 1 g
% calories from fat: 37
Carbohydrates: 28 g
Protein: 5 g
Cholesterol: 0 mg
Sodium: 226 mg

Spray the grill with the cooking spray and preheat for 5 minutes. Place the mushroom slices on the grill and drizzle with 1 tablespoon olive oil and 1 teaspoon balsamic vinegar. Sprinkle with half of the pepper and seasoned salt. Grill for 4 minutes. Place the onion and green pepper slices on top of the mushroom slices, drizzle with the remaining oil and vinegar and season with the remaining pepper and salt. Grill for 3 to 4 minutes. Toast the rolls under the broiler and then evenly distribute the grilled vegetables and portobello mushrooms onto the rolls for each sandwich. Garnish the grilled vegetables with the fresh Italian parsley. Serves 4.

Quick & Easy Savory Steak Sandwiches

1 lb. lean chuck steak
1 T. butter, melted
2 T. lemon juice
1 T. Worcestershire sauce
1 clove garlic, minced
1 T. ketchup
salt and pepper to taste

nonfat cooking spray
4 hero sandwich rolls
prepared mustard
nonfat mayonnaise
4 slices sweet onion
4 slices ripe tomato
8 romaine lettuce leaves

Remove any excess fat from the chuck steak and slice across the grain into thin strips. In a medium bowl, whisk together the butter, lemon juice, Worcestershire sauce, garlic, ketchup and the salt and pepper to taste. Place the meat strips in the sauce. Spray the grill with cooking spray and preheat the grill for 5 minutes. Place the meat strips on the grill and cook for 4 to 5 minutes. Spread the prepared mustard on one side of each roll, and the mayonnaise on the other side. To serve, place the grilled meat evenly on the rolls and top with the onion slices, tomato slices and the lettuce leaves. Serves 4.

NUTRITIONAL ANALYSIS:

Calories: 396
Total fat: 15 g
Saturated fat: 5 g
% calories from fat: 32
Carbohydrates: 39 g
Protein: 31 g
Cholesterol: 75 mg
Sodium: 549 mg

Herbed Tuna & Provolone Rolls

6 oz. can white tuna, water packed
1/2 c. soft bread crumbs
1 egg white
1 t. fresh basil, minced
1 t. fresh parsley, minced
1/4 c. prepared chili sauce

1/4 t. ground black pepper
1/4 t. garlic salt
4 kaiser rolls, sliced
4 slices provolone cheese
8 romaine lettuce leaves
nonfat cooking spray

Drain the tuna and flake it into a medium bowl. Mix the tuna with the bread crumbs, egg white, basil, parsley, chili sauce, black pepper and the garlic salt. Spray the grill with the cooking spray and preheat for 5 minutes. Shape the tuna mixture into 4 patties. Place the patties on the grill and cook for 4 to 5 minutes. Place the tuna patties on the rolls and top with the provolone cheese and lettuce leaves. Serves 4.

NUTRITIONAL ANALYSIS:

Calories: 395
Total fat: 12 g
Saturated fat: 6 g
% calories from fat: 27
Carbohydrates: 46 g
Protein: 27 g
Cholesterol: 42 mg
Sodium: 1452 mg

14

Enchilada Cheese Quesadillas

4 lowfat flour tortillas
1/2 c. prepared enchilada sauce
1 c. pepper Jack cheese, shredded
2 T. green onions, chopped

3 T. sliced black olives
1 T. fresh cilantro, chopped
nonfat cooking spray

Liberally brush one side of each of the flour tortillas with the enchilada sauce. Evenly divide the cheese between the tortillas, spreading the cheese on only half of each tortilla. Top each layer of cheese with green onions, black olives and the cilantro. Fold the empty half of the tortilla over the cheese mixture. Spray the grill with cooking spray and preheat for 5 minutes. Place one filled tortilla onto the grill and cook for 2 to 3 minutes, until lightly browned. Remove the grilled quesadilla and grill the remaining quesadillas. Serves 4.

NUTRITIONAL ANALYSIS:
Calories: 254
Total fat: 11 g
Saturated fat: 5 g
% calories from fat: 39
Carbohydrates: 29 g
Protein: 11 g
Cholesterol: 18 mg
Sodium: 806 mg

Summertime Fruit Skewers with Cinnamon-Sugar

1 tart baking apple, peeled and cut into
   1-inch chunks
2 plums, peeled and cut into 1-inch chunks
2 peaches, peeled and cut into 1-inch
   chunks
3 T. lowfat butter, melted

2 T. sugar
1 t. ground cinnamon
8 10-inch long bamboo skewers, soaked in
   water
nonfat cooking spray

NUTRITIONAL ANALYSIS:

Calories: 147
Total fat: 5 g
Saturated fat: 3 g
% calories from fat: 28
Carbohydrates: 28 g
Protein: 1 g
Cholesterol: 15 mg
Sodium: 53 mg

Thread the fruit onto the skewers, alternating the different fruits. In a small bowl, combine the butter, sugar and cinnamon until the sugar has dissolved. Spray the grill with the cooking spray and preheat for 5 minutes. Place the skewers on the grill horizontally and brush each piece of fruit with the butter and cinnamon–sugar mixture. Grill the fruit for 2 to 3 minutes. Serves 4.

Grilled "Fried" Potato Spears

2 russet potatoes
1 T. vegetable oil
1 t. cider vinegar
1 T. fresh parsley, minced

1/2 t. ground black pepper
1 t. seasoned salt
nonfat cooking spray

Scrub the potatoes and remove any blemishes. Cut each potato into fries, about ½-inch thick and 4-inches in length. Sprinkle the oil and cider vinegar over the potatoes and let them stand for 5 minutes. Spray the grill with cooking spray and preheat for 5 minutes. Place the potato spears onto the grill horizontally. Sprinkle with the parsley, black pepper and the seasoned salt. Grill for 7 to 9 minutes. Serves 4.

NUTRITIONAL ANALYSIS:

Calories: 80
Total fat: 3 g
Saturated fat: <1 g
% calories from fat: 36
Carbohydrates: 10 g
Protein: 4 g
Cholesterol: 0 mg
Sodium: 253 mg

CHAPTER 3

Great Grilled Beef

Grilled beef is the perfect choice when you are looking for stellar flavor, balanced textures and tantalizing aromas. Beef grilled in the George Foreman® Lean Mean Fat Reducing Grilling Machine is quick to prepare and the delicious results will be enjoyed by everyone in the family. The patented grids of the grill provide superior grilling and the construction of the grill allows the fat to channel away into the Drip Tray.

When you only have a few moments to prepare and grill dinner, try *Lemon-Garlic Rubbed Sirloin Steaks, Rosemary Butter London Broil* or *Sizzling Hot Tenderloin Steaks.* Each is ready to serve in less than 30 minutes. For inviting family meals, choose *Caribbean Beef Kebabs, Tex-Mex Steak Fajitas* or *Family-Style BBQ Beef Ribs.* Kids will particularly enjoy building their own fajitas and eating ribs and kebabs in a casual setting.

Because beef can be heavy in fat, look for the

lean cuts of beef at your grocery store and choose the most lean ground beef you can find. Use about ¼ pound of beef per person for smaller and more healthful portions. One of the nicest features of the George Foreman® Lean Mean Fat Reducing Grilling Machine is that you don't have to lose flavor when you lose the fat and the recipes in this chapter are designed to give you the best flavor, using fresh herbs and spices, fresh vegetables and light marinades and rubs. Enjoy!

Zesty Dijon Beef Tri-Tip

1/2 c. low sodium soy sauce
3/4 c. balsamic vinegar
2 T. extra virgin olive oil
2 T. lowfat Dijon mustard
3 cloves garlic, minced

1 t. pepper
2 habañero peppers, seeded and minced
3 tabasco peppers, minced
2 lbs. beef tri-tip roast
nonfat cooking spray

NUTRITIONAL ANALYSIS:

Calories: 296
Total fat: 18 g
Saturated fat: 6 g
% calories from fat: 57
Carbohydrates: 7 g
Protein: 23 g
Cholesterol: 74 mg
Sodium: 1222 mg

Coat the grill with cooking spray and preheat for 5 minutes. In a small bowl, combine all of the ingredients except the roast. Blend well. Remove any visible fat from the roast and slice thinly across the grain. Place the slices of roast on the grill and brush with the basting sauce. Grill for 2 minutes. Brush with the sauce again and grill an additional 3 to 5 minutes. Serves 6 to 8.

Caribbean Beef Kebabs

1 lb. beef sirloin, visible fat removed
2 T. vegetable oil
4 cloves garlic, roughly chopped
1 large purple onion, roughly chopped
2 habañero peppers, seeded and chopped
2 T. fresh parsley, chopped
1/4 c. cider vinegar
2 T. dark brown sugar, packed

1/4 t. ground cinnamon
1/8 t. ground cloves
1 t. ground allspice
1/4 c. fresh lime juice
8 10-inch wooden skewers, soaked in water
    and drained
nonfat cooking spray

Cut the beef into 1-inch cubes. Set aside. Combine all of the ingredients except the beef and process in a blender for 2 minutes, or until smooth. Place the cubed beef in a glass pan and pour the sauce over the beef. Cover and marinate in the refrigerator for 2 hours or up to 6 hours.

Coat the grill with cooking spray and preheat 5 minutes. Thread the meat evenly onto 8 skewers. Place the beef skewers on the grill widthwise (horizontally) and cook 8 to 9 minutes. Serves 4.

NUTRITIONAL ANALYSIS:
Calories: 351
Total fat: 22g
Saturated fat: 7 g
% calories from fat: 56
Carbohydrates: 15 g
Protein: 23 g
Cholesterol: 75 mg
Sodium: 66 mg

Lemon-Garlic Rubbed Sirloin Steaks

1 lb. beef sirloin steak
3 cloves garlic, finely minced
1 t. ketchup
1 t. cracked black pepper

1/2 t. salt
2 T. lemon juice
1 T. olive oil
nonfat cooking spray

Coat the grill with cooking spray and preheat for 5 minutes. Remove any visible fat from the steak. In a small bowl, combine the garlic, ketchup, pepper, salt, lemon juice and olive oil.

Mix to make a thick paste. Generously press the rub onto all sides of the steak. Place the steak in the grill and cook for 7 to 9 minutes. Serves 4.

NUTRITIONAL ANALYSIS:
Calories: **269**
Total fat: **18 g**
Saturated fat: **6 g**
% calories from fat: **63**
Carbohydrates: **2 g**
Protein: **22 g**
Cholesterol: **75 mg**
Sodium: **368 mg**

Tex-Mex Steak Fajitas

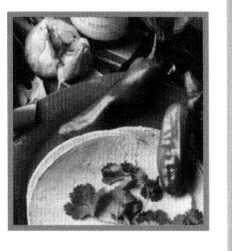

1/2 lb. beef flank steak
1/3 c. fresh lime juice
1/4 c. prepared chili sauce
1/4 c. vegetable oil
1 small, white onion, chopped
1/4 c. fresh cilantro, chopped
1/8 t. chili powder
1/2 t. ground cumin

1/2 t. salt
1/2 t. black pepper
1 green pepper
1 red pepper
8 lowfat fajita-sized flour tortillas
1/2 c. lowfat cheddar cheese
1/2 c. nonfat sour cream
nonfat cooking spray

Remove any visible fat from the steak. Cut the steak into very thin slices across the grain of the meat and place in a flat glass pan. Mix together the lime juice, chili sauce, oil, onion, cilantro, chili powder, cumin, salt and pepper and pour over the steak. Refrigerate for 2 to 4 hours. Remove the seeds and inner fibers from the green and red peppers and cut into thin slices. Coat the grill with cooking spray and preheat for 5 minutes. Discard the marinade and grill the steak for 3 minutes. Add the peppers over the top of the steak and grill for 4 to 5 minutes. To serve, fill warm tortillas with the meat and vegetables. Add cheese and sour cream as desired. Serves 8.

NUTRITIONAL ANALYSIS:

Calories: 281
Total fat: 10 g
Saturated fat: 2 g
% calories from fat: 32
Carbohydrates: 35 g
Protein: 13 g
Cholesterol: 17 mg
Sodium: 825 mg

Milano-Stuffed Flank Steak

2 lbs. beef flank steak
2 c. fresh tomato, chopped
2 T. fresh parsley, finely minced
2 cloves garlic, finely minced
1/2 c. sweet onion, chopped
1/4 c. green pepper, chopped

1/4 c. zucchini, finely chopped
1 T. fresh sage, finely chopped
1/2 t. black pepper
1/2 t. salt
1 T. extra virgin olive oil
nonfat cooking spray

NUTRITIONAL ANALYSIS:
Calories: 278
Total fat: 14 g
Saturated fat: 5 g
% calories from fat: 46
Carbohydrates: 5 g
Protein: 32 g
Cholesterol: 76 mg
Sodium: 311 mg

Remove any visible fat from the steak. With a sharp knife, cut a slit sideways into the steak to create a pocket, without cutting completely through the meat. In a medium bowl, combine the tomato, parsley, garlic, onion, green pepper, zucchini, sage, pepper, salt and olive oil. Toss to coat the vegetables completely. Stuff the pocket of the steak with the vegetable–herb mixture. Press the sides of the steak to close or secure with toothpicks, if desired. Coat the grill with cooking spray and preheat for 5 minutes. Grill the stuffed steak for 9 to 11 minutes, or according to your taste. To serve, cut the steak across the grain into ¼–inch slices, carefully preserving the vegetables inside. Top the slices with any remaining vegetable mixture. Serves 6.

Family-Style BBQ Beef Ribs

5 lbs. beef short ribs
1/2 c. tomato sauce
1/4 c. dark brown sugar, packed
1 T. cider vinegar
1 T. Worcestershire sauce

2 T. prepared mustard
1 clove garlic, finely minced
1 T. chili powder
1 t. salt
nonfat cooking spray

Parboil the ribs for 20 minutes. (To parboil ribs: cook the ribs for 20 minutes in a steamer rack over a pan of boiling water). Cool and remove any visible fat from the ribs. Coat the grill with the cooking spray and preheat for 5 minutes. In a small bowl, combine the tomato sauce, brown sugar, vinegar, Worcestershire sauce, mustard, garlic, chili powder and salt. Grill the ribs for 3 minutes and baste with sauce. Grill for an additional 2 minutes and baste again, turning the ribs to coat thoroughly. Grill an additional 2 minutes. Serve the ribs with any remaining sauce. Serves 6.

NUTRITIONAL ANALYSIS:

Calories: 421
Total fat: 24 g
Saturated fat: 10 g
% calories from fat: 51
Carbohydrates: 7 g
Protein: 44 g
Cholesterol: 134 mg
Sodium: 499 mg

Rosemary Butter London Broil

1 1/2 lbs. beef London broil steak, 1 1/2-inch thick
1/2 c. lowfat unsalted margarine
1 clove garlic, minced
1 t. paprika

1 T. fresh rosemary, finely minced
1 t. salt
2 T. green onions, finely chopped
1 t. black pepper

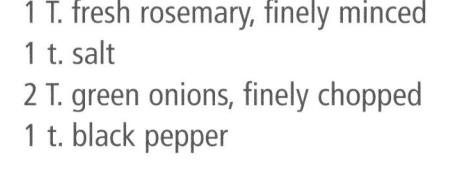

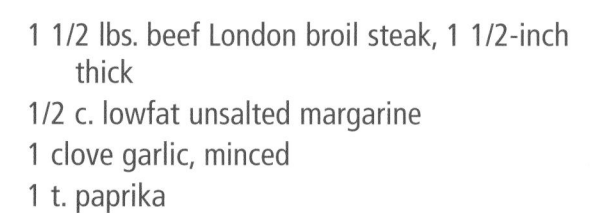

NUTRITIONAL ANALYSIS:

Calories: 267
Total fat: 18 g
Saturated fat: 5 g
% calories from fat: 61
Carbohydrates: 1 g
Protein: 25 g
Cholesterol: 67 mg
Sodium: 446 mg

Coat the grill with cooking spray and preheat for 5 minutes. In a small bowl, combine the margarine, garlic, paprika, rosemary, salt, green onions and black pepper. Blend well. Remove any visible fat from the steak and grill the steak for 3 minutes. Brush the butter–herb sauce over the steak and grill for an additional 4 to 5 minutes. As the butter sauce melts, it will run into the drip tray. To serve, slice the beef thinly across the grain and arrange on a warm serving platter. Pour the melted butter sauce from the drip tray over the sliced beef. Serves 6.

Sizzling Hot Tenderloin Steaks

4 4 oz. beef tenderloin steaks
1/4 c. sugar
2 cloves garlic, minced
1 T. paprika
3 T. black pepper
2 T. chili powder

1 t. ground ginger
1 t. onion powder
1 t. ground coriander
1 t. cayenne pepper
nonfat cooking spray

Coat the grill with cooking spray and preheat for 5 minutes. Combine the sugar, garlic, paprika, pepper, chili powder, ginger, onion powder, coriander and cayenne in a small bowl.

Remove any visible fat from the steaks. Place the steaks in the grill and cook for 4 minutes. Sprinkle heavily with the spices and grill an additional 1 to 2 minutes. Serves 4.

NUTRITIONAL ANALYSIS:

Calories: **400**
Total fat: **26 g**
Saturated fat: **10 g**
% calories from fat: **58**
Carbohydrates: **20 g**
Protein: **23 g**
Cholesterol: **79 mg**
Sodium: **95 mg**

Ginger Grilled Beef & Rice Bowls

2 6 oz. ribeye steaks
1 T. brown sugar
1/2 T. rice vinegar
2 cloves garlic, finely minced
1 t. ground ginger
1 t. dry mustard powder

1 T. Worcestershire sauce
1 t. fresh lemon juice
2 t. black pepper
4 c. cooked long-grain white rice
nonfat cooking spray

NUTRITIONAL ANALYSIS:

Calories: 470
Total fat: 20 g
Saturated fat: 8 g
% calories from fat: 39
Carbohydrates: 50 g
Protein: 20 g
Cholesterol: 58 mg
Sodium: 93 mg

Remove any visible fat from the steaks and place the steaks in a flat glass pan. Combine the brown sugar, vinegar, garlic, ginger, mustard powder, Worcestershire sauce, lemon juice and black pepper in a medium bowl and mix well. Pour the marinade over the steaks and chill for at least 1 hour in the refrigerator.

Coat the grill with the cooking spray and preheat for 5 minutes. Grill the steaks for 5 to 7 minutes, or according to your preference. To serve, thinly slice the beef and place it on top of the hot cooked rice. Top with a drizzle of juice from the drip tray. Serves 4.

Mediterranean Steak Salad

1 lb. beef flank steak
1/4 c. balsamic vinegar
1 t. black pepper, coarsely ground
1 t. garlic salt
2 T. vegetable oil
8 c. mixed salad greens, crisped in the
    refrigerator

1 small cucumber, peeled and sliced
1 ripe beefsteak tomato, sliced
1 small red onion, sliced thin
1 green pepper, cored, seeded and sliced
nonfat cooking spray

Remove any visible fat from the beef. In a small bowl, mix together the vinegar, pepper, garlic salt and oil. Lightly coat the grill with cooking spray and preheat for 5 minutes. Place the beef in the grill and cook for 4 minutes. Sprinkle the steak with the vinegar dressing, reserving some of the dressing for the salad topping. Grill the steak for an additional 3 to 4 minutes. Cut the cooked beef into very thin slices across the grain. To serve, mound the greens on 4 individual salad plates. Layer evenly on all 4 plates the cucumber, tomato, red onion and green pepper. Top the salad with the desired amount of sliced beef. Drizzle the remaining dressing over the salads. Serves 4.

NUTRITIONAL ANALYSIS:

Calories: 379
Total fat: 16 g
Saturated fat: 5 g
% calories from fat: 39
Carbohydrates: 22 g
Protein: 32 g
Cholesterol: 57 mg
Sodium: 1529 mg

Honey Mustard Beef Tenderloin

4 4 oz. tenderloin steaks
2 T. prepared Dijon mustard
2 T. pure honey
1 T. fresh lime juice
1 clove garlic, minced

2 T. sesame oil
1/4 t. salt
1 t. black pepper
nonfat cooking oil

Remove any visible fat from the beef and place the steaks in a glass pan. Combine the mustard, honey, lime juice, garlic, oil, salt and pepper and pour over the steaks. Cover and refrigerate for 4 to 12 hours. Coat the grill with cooking spray and preheat for 5 minutes. Place the steaks on the grill for 5 to 7 minutes. Slice the steaks into thick slices and serve on a warmed platter. Serves 4.

NUTRITIONAL ANALYSIS:

Calories: 418
Total fat: 32 g
Saturated fat: 10 g
% calories from fat: 71
Carbohydrates: 9 g
Protein: 21 g
Cholesterol: 80 mg
Sodium: 381 mg

50 Great George Foreman® Lean Mean Fat Reducing Grilling Machine Recipes!

CHAPTER 4

Great Grilled Pork & Lamb

Lean cuts of pork tenderloin and pork chops can be delightfully paired with a wide variety of sauces, marinades and rubs. Pork has a fine, even texture and a mild flavor that is also easily adaptable to creative grilling recipes, such as the recipes in this chapter. Smoked pork and hams tend to carry higher amounts of fat, so look for boneless ham that has been smoked without additional fat and read the meat labels carefully. When preparing pork, remember to test the meat with a meat thermometer before removing from the grill. Use a meat thermometer that registers at least 150° to 160°F so that harmful bacteria will be eliminated.

Pork is a delightful change of pace and your family will enjoy these special entrées.

Chinese Hoisin-Sauced Pork Chops with Fresh Cilantro

4 to 6 6 oz. boneless pork chops
1/2 c. hoisin sauce
1/2 c. low-sodium soy sauce
1/4 c. white vinegar
1/4 c. honey

1/4 c. pineapple juice
2 cloves garlic, minced
fresh cilantro sprigs for garnish
nonfat cooking spray

NUTRITIONAL ANALYSIS:

Calories: 315
Total fat: 13 g
Saturated fat: 4 g
% calories from fat: 38
Carbohydrates: 24 g
Protein: 25 g
Cholesterol: 66 mg
Sodium: 1101 mg

Remove any visible fat from the pork tenderloin chops. In a sealable plastic bag, combine thoroughly the hoisin sauce, soy sauce, white vinegar, honey, pineapple juice and the garlic. Place the pork chops in the bag and cover them completely with the marinade. Marinate in the refrigerator for 2 to 12 hours. Remove the meat and discard the marinade. Spray the grill with the cooking spray and preheat for 5 minutes. Grill the pork chops for 5 to 6 minutes, or according to your preference. Garnish each tenderloin chop with the fresh cilantro sprigs. Serves 4 to 6.

Bacon & Mushroom Stuffed Pork Chops

4 to 6 pork loin chops, 1-inch thick
4 slices turkey bacon
1/4 c. white onion, minced
1 clove garlic, minced
1 c. white button mushrooms, chopped

1/8 t. ground black pepper
2 T. balsamic-flavored olive oil
salt and black pepper to taste
nonfat cooking spray

Remove any excess fat on the pork chops. Using a sharp knife, cut a deep pocket into the center of each chop without cutting all the way through the pork. Salt and pepper the chops to taste. Set aside. Using a skillet, sauté the bacon until crisp. Remove the bacon to a paper towel and then crumble. Pour off the bacon fat in the skillet except for 1 teaspoon. Heat the skillet and add the onion and garlic and sauté until the onion is translucent. Add the mushrooms and continue sautéing until the mushrooms are tender. Remove the skillet from the heat and stir in the black pepper and the crumbled bacon. Stuff each pork chop with the mushroom and bacon filling. Use a toothpick to close the pocket edges. Lightly brush both sides of the pork chops with the balsamic-flavored oil. Spray the grill with the cooking spray and preheat for 5 minutes. Grill the stuffed pork chops for 6 to 8 minutes, or until the pork is completely cooked. Serves 4 to 6.

NUTRITIONAL ANALYSIS:

Calories: 216
Total fat: 16 g
Saturated fat: 4 g
% calories from fat: 66
Carbohydrates: 1 g
Protein: 17 g
Cholesterol: 57 mg
Sodium: 198 mg

Grilled Ham Steaks with Fresh Citrus Marinade

1 1/2 lbs. lowfat ham steak, fully cooked
1 t. orange rind, grated
1 c. fresh orange juice
1/4 c. low-sodium soy sauce
2 T. sesame oil

1 T. sugar
1/4 t. salt
1/8 t. ground black pepper
2 T. fresh chives, chopped
nonfat cooking spray

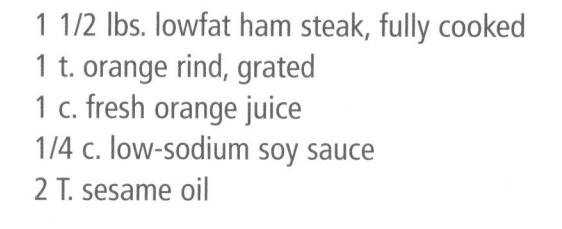

NUTRITIONAL ANALYSIS:

Calories: 223
Total fat: 10 g
Saturated fat: 2 g
% calories from fat: 39
Carbohydrates: 10 g
Protein: 23 g
Cholesterol: 51 mg
Sodium: 1891 mg

Remove any excess fat from the ham steak and cut it into 6 equal portions. In a sealable plastic bag or in a non-reactive pan, combine the orange rind, orange juice, soy sauce, oil, sugar, salt, pepper and the chives until blended. Add the ham steaks and refrigerate for 2 hours.

Remove the ham steaks from the marinade and discard the marinade. Spray the grill with the nonfat cooking spray and preheat for 5 minutes. Grill the ham steaks for 3 to 4 minutes, until heated through. Serves 6.

Glazed Pork & Fruit Kebab Duo

1 lb. pork tenderloin
1 c. apricot preserves
1/2 c. water
2 T. butter, melted
1/4 c. lime juice
1 t. ground cinnamon
1/4 t. ground cloves

2 large oranges, cut into 16 wedges with the peel
16 small cubes honeydew melon or cantaloupe
1 pear, cut into 16 cubes, with or without the skin
8 10-inch wooden skewers, soaked in water
nonfat cooking spray

Cut the tenderloin into 1-inch cubes and place the cubes into a non-reactive bowl. In a separate small bowl, whisk together the apricot preserves, water, butter, juice, cinnamon and the cloves until smooth. Pour half of the sauce over the cubes of pork. Cover the pork and refrigerate for 2 to 4 hours. Keep the reserved sauce refrigerated until grilling time. Remove the pork cubes from the marinade and discard the marinade. Thread the pork alternately with the fruit cubes onto the skewers. Spray the grill with the cooking spray and preheat for 5 minutes. Place the kebabs on the grill horizontally and brush with the refrigerated reserved sauce. Grill for 6 to 8 minutes, or until the pork is cooked to your preference. Serves 4.

NUTRITIONAL ANALYSIS:
Calories: 498
Total fat: 12 g
Saturated fat: 6 g
% calories from fat: 22
Carbohydrates: 77 g
Protein: 25 g
Cholesterol: 90 mg
Sodium: 152 mg

Asian Grilled Pork Lo Mein

1 lb. pork tenderloin, cut into thin slices
1/4 c. ketchup
2 T. hoisin sauce
1 t. oyster sauce
1/4 c. honey
1 T. garlic, minced
1 T. fresh cilantro, chopped
1/2 t. salt
nonfat cooking spray

2 T. vegetable oil
1/2 c. carrot, thinly sliced
1/2 c. green bell pepper, thinly sliced
1/2 c. fresh bean sprouts, cleaned and cut
into 1-inch lengths
1 to 1 1/2 c. prepared stir-fry sauce
8 oz. Chinese egg noodles, cooked and
drained

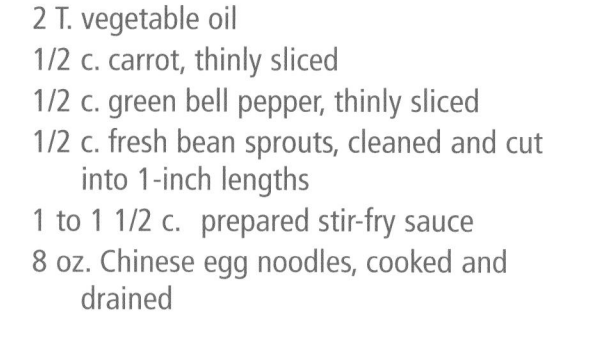

NUTRITIONAL ANALYSIS:

Calories: 439
Total fat: 21 g
Saturated fat: 4 g
% calories from fat: 41
Carbohydrates: 45 g
Protein: 20 g
Cholesterol: 50 mg
Sodium: 891 mg

In a sealable plastic bag, combine the ketchup, hoisin sauce, oyster sauce, honey, garlic, cilantro and the salt. Add the tenderloin slices and marinate for 4 to 12 hours. Spray the grill with the cooking spray and preheat for 5 minutes. Remove the slices of pork from the marinade, discard the marinade and grill the pork for 3 to 5 minutes. In a large skillet, sauté the vegetables in the oil until just tender. Add the grilled pork and the stir-fry sauce to the vegetables, mix well and then gently stir in the cooked noodles. Serves 6.

50 Great George Foreman® Lean Mean Fat Reducing Grilling Machine Recipes!

Spicy Grilled Pork & Red Potatoes

4 6 oz. pork chops
1 lb. small red potatoes, scrubbed and cut
 into small wedges
4 T. prepared mustard
1 t. dark brown sugar

1/2 t. prepared horseradish
3/4 c. chili sauce
2 T. cider vinegar
nonfat cooking spray

Remove any excess fat from the pork chops. Place the chops in a glass pan and place the red potatoes in a sealable plastic bag. In a small bowl, whisk together the mustard, brown sugar, horseradish, chili sauce and the vinegar until blended. Pour half of the sauce over the meat. Cover the meat and pour the remaining sauce over the potatoes. Marinate both the meat and the potatoes for 2 to 4 hours. Spray the grill with the cooking spray and preheat for 5 minutes. Place the potatoes on the grill and cook for 4 minutes. Push the potatoes to the sides of the grill and add the pork chops. Grill for 5 to 6 minutes. Serves 4.

NUTRITIONAL ANALYSIS:

Calories: 446
Total fat: 23 g
Saturated fat: 7 g
% calories from fat: 46
Carbohydrates: 23 g
Protein: 37 g
Cholesterol: 114 mg
Sodium: 1712 mg

50 Great George Foreman® Lean Mean Fat Reducing Grilling Machine Recipes!

37

Chili-Lime Pork Tenderloin

1 1/2 lbs. pork tenderloin
1/4 c. lowfat butter
3 T. fresh lime juice
2 t. chili powder

1 t. lime rind, grated
1/2 t. garlic salt
1/4 t. ground black pepper
nonfat cooking spray

Remove any excess fat from the pork tenderloin. Cut the tenderloin into four steaks. In a small saucepan over low heat, melt the butter. Cool slightly and whisk in the lime juice, chili powder, lime rind, garlic salt and the black pepper. Spray the grill with the cooking spray and preheat for 5 minutes. Liberally brush one side of each steak with the butter sauce and place the steaks on the grill, sauced–side down. Brush the remaining butter sauce on the top of the steaks and close the lid. The butter sauce will run into the drip tray as the pork steaks grill. Grill for 5 to 6 minutes, or until cooked as desired. Serves 4.

NUTRITIONAL ANALYSIS:
Calories: 290
Total fat: 15 g
Saturated fat: 7 g
% calories from fat: 48
Carbohydrates: 2 g
Protein: 35 g
Cholesterol: 132 mg
Sodium: 329 mg

50 Great George Foreman® Lean Mean Fat Reducing Grilling Machine Recipes!

Dijon Mustard & Dill Pork Chops

4 6 oz. pork chops
1/4 c. white vinegar
1/4 c. lemon juice
1 T. extra virgin olive oil
2 T. Dijon mustard

1 clove garlic, minced
2 T. dried dill weed
2 T. fresh parsley, chopped
nonfat cooking spray

Remove any excess fat from the pork chops. In a sealable plastic bag, combine the vinegar, lemon juice, olive oil, Dijon mustard, garlic, dill weed and the parsley. Add the pork chops and marinate in the refrigerator for 2 to 4 hours.

Spray the grill with the cooking spray and preheat for 5 minutes. Remove the pork chops from the marinade and discard the marinade. Place the chops on the grill and cook for 5 to 6 minutes, or until grilled as desired. Serves 4.

NUTRITIONAL ANALYSIS:
Calories: 391
Total fat: 25 g
Saturated fat: 8 g
% calories from fat: 60
Carbohydrates: 3 g
Protein: 35 g
Cholesterol: 114 mg
Sodium: 287 mg

Grilled Lamb & Beefsteak Tomatoes

4 boneless lamb chops, about 6 ounces each
1 t. fresh thyme, minced
1 t. fresh parsley, minced
splash balsamic vinegar

1/4 t. black pepper
4 large ripe beefsteak tomatoes, cored and
   thickly sliced

Preheat the grill for 5 minutes. Place the lamb chops in the grill and dust with half of the thyme, parsley, vinegar and pepper. Cook for 5 to 6 minutes. Remove to a warmed platter. Add the tomatoes to the grill and dust with the remaining thyme, parsley, vinegar and pepper. Grill for 3 minutes, or until softened and warm. To serve, mound the tomatoes over the lamb and serve while hot. Serves 4.

NUTRITIONAL ANALYSIS:
Calories: 263
Total fat: 9 g
Saturated fat: 3 g
% calories from fat: 31
Carbohydrates: 9 g
Protein: 36 g
Cholesterol: 109 mg
Sodium: 125 mg

50 Great George Foreman® Lean Mean Fat Reducing Grilling Machine Recipes!

Greek Lamb Salata with Oregano Dressing

2 boneless lamb loin chops, excess fat
   removed
1 t. lemon juice
1/2 t. salt
1/4 t. black pepper
1 head romaine lettuce, torn into bite-sized
   pieces
3 plum tomatoes, washed and chopped
1 purple onion, peeled and cut into thin rings
1 green bell pepper, seeded and sliced

1 c. Greek kalamata olives
1/4 lb. feta cheese, crumbled

Oregano Dressing
2 T. extra virgin olive oil
2 T. water
2 T. red vinegar
pinch ground oregano
salt and pepper to taste

Preheat the grill for 5 minutes. Place the lamb in the grill and sprinkle with the lemon juice. Dust the chops with the salt and pepper. Grill for 5 to 6 minutes. Remove from the grill and slice the lamb into thin strips.

To assemble the salad, combine the lettuce, tomatoes, onion, green pepper, olives and feta cheese. Whisk together in a deep bowl, the olive oil, water, vinegar, oregano, salt and pepper. Layer the lamb slices over the salad, dress and serve. Serves 4.

NUTRITIONAL ANALYSIS:
Calories: 396
Total fat: 23 g
Saturated fat: 8 g
% calories from fat: 52
Carbohydrates: 18 g
Protein: 31 g
Cholesterol: 98 mg
Sodium: 1038 mg

50 Great George Foreman® Lean Mean Fat Reducing Grilling Machine Recipes!

41

Great Grilled Poultry

One of the best features of the George Foreman® Lean Mean Fat Reducing Grilling Machine is that it quickly and effortlessly grills boneless chicken breasts to perfection. In this chapter, we've combined several delightful ingredients to get you started on your own creative poultry recipes.

Whenever poultry is grilled, it should be cooked thoroughly until no pink remains. A meat thermometer should register 180°F in order to completely eliminate any harmful bacteria.

Because poultry is so versatile, you can include it with just about any sauce, marinade, rub or salsa and it will be adaptable to your favorite recipes!

Fiery Sweet Grilled Chicken Breasts

4 boneless, skinless chicken breast halves
2 T. low sodium soy sauce
2 T. hoisin sauce
2 T. chili sauce
1/4 c. honey

1/4 c. vinegar
3 cloves garlic, minced
1/2 t. chili powder
1/2 t. black pepper
nonfat cooking spray

Place the chicken breasts in a large glass pan. In a separate bowl, mix together the soy sauce, hoisin sauce, chili sauce, honey, vinegar, garlic, chili powder and black pepper. Completely cover the chicken with the sauce and refrigerate for 2 hours or up to 6 hours. Lightly coat the grill with cooking spray and preheat for 5 minutes. Place the chicken in the grill and cook for 5 to 7 minutes, or until no pink remains. Serves 4.

NUTRITIONAL ANALYSIS:

Calories: 178
Total fat: 1 g
Saturated fat: >1 g
% calories from fat: 6
Carbohydrates: 25 g
Protein: 17 g
Cholesterol: 41 mg
Sodium: 719 mg

Lemon-Orange Rubbed Chicken Breasts

2 T. lowfat margarine
1/4 c. fresh lemon juice
1/4 c. light brown sugar, packed
1/4 c. frozen orange juice concentrate
2 t. orange zest, minced

1/2 t. ground mace
1/2 t. salt
1/2 t. ground black pepper
4 boneless, skinless chicken breast halves
nonfat cooking spray

NUTRITIONAL ANALYSIS:

Calories: 191
Total fat: 4 g
Saturated fat: 1 g
% calories from fat: 18
Carbohydrates: 22 g
Protein: 17 g
Cholesterol: 41 mg
Sodium: 381 mg

Combine the margarine, lemon juice and brown sugar in mixing bowl. Mix until smooth. Blend in the orange juice, zest, mace, salt and pepper. Mix well. Cover the chicken completely with the wet rub. Coat the grill with cooking spray and preheat for 5 minutes. Grill the chicken for 5 to 7 minutes, or until no pink remains. Serves 4.

Pineapple & Honey Stuffed Chicken Breasts

4 boneless, skinless chicken breast halves
1 c. pineapple chunks, diced fine
1/2 c. pineapple juice
1/4 c. fresh lime juice
2 T. low sodium soy sauce
2 T. canola oil

2 T. honey
3 cloves garlic, minced
1/2 t. black pepper
1 t. fresh cilantro, minced
nonfat cooking spray

Place the chicken on a clean cutting surface. With the tip of a sharp knife, slit each breast open without cutting through the entire breast, to create a pocket. In a medium bowl, mix together the pineapple, pineapple juice, lime juice, soy sauce, oil, honey, garlic, pepper and cilantro. Pack one fourth of the stuffing into each chicken breast and press the edges of the chicken breast together to close the pocket. A small bit of the pineapple may spill out slightly during grilling, but this will not affect the outcome of the chicken. Lightly coat the grill with the cooking spray and preheat for 5 minutes. Grill the stuffed chicken for 7 to 9 minutes, or until the chicken is fully cooked and the stuffing is warm. Scoop up any excess pineapple with the plastic spatula and serve with the chicken. Serves 4.

NUTRITIONAL ANALYSIS:
Calories: 216
Total fat: 8 g
Saturated fat: 1 g
% calories from fat: 32
Carbohydrates: 19 g
Protein: 17 g
Cholesterol: 41 mg
Sodium: 348 mg

Grilled Parmesan Chicken with Angel Hair Pasta

2 boneless skinless chicken breasts
2 T. extra virgin olive oil
3 cloves garlic, finely minced
2 T. fresh parsley, finely minced
1 t. ground oregano
1 t. dried basil

1/4 c. Parmesan cheese, grated
1 t. black pepper, coarsely ground
1/2 t. salt
10 oz. angel hair pasta, cooked al dente and
  drained
nonfat cooking spray

**NUTRITIONAL
ANALYSIS:**

Calories: 390
Total fat: 11 g
Saturated fat: 2 g
% calories from fat: 25
Carbohydrates: 52 g
Protein: 21 g
Cholesterol: 26 mg
Sodium: 444 mg

Remove any visible fat from the chicken. Slice the chicken thinly across the grain of the meat. In a small bowl, combine the oil, garlic, parsley, oregano, basil, Parmesan cheese, pepper and salt. Coat the grill with the cooking spray and preheat for 5 minutes. Grill the chicken slices for 3 to 4 minutes or until fully cooked. Place the pasta on a serving platter, pour the sauce over and toss well. Arrange the chicken slices on top and serve immediately. Serves 4.

Polynesian Glazed Turkey Medallions

2 lbs. boneless, skinless turkey breast
   medallions
1/4 c. extra virgin olive oil
2 green onions, finely minced
1/4 t. crushed red chili peppers

1/2 c. cider vinegar
2 c. orange juice
1 T. light brown sugar
1 T. honey
nonfat cooking spray

In a medium bowl, combine the oil, onions, red peppers, vinegar, orange juice, brown sugar and honey. Coat the grill with cooking spray and preheat for 5 minutes. Place the medallions on the grill and spoon 1 tablespoon of the glaze over the turkey. Grill for 2 minutes. Open the grill lid and spoon the glaze over the turkey again. Grill for another 2 minutes and baste again. Grill for 1 additional minute, or until no pink remains, and serve. Serves 6.

NUTRITIONAL ANALYSIS:

Calories: 311
Total fat: 10 g
Saturated fat: 2 g
% calories from fat: 31
Carbohydrates: 15 g
Protein: 37 g
Cholesterol: 100 mg
Sodium: 83 mg

Turkey Medallions in Lemon-Herb Marinade

1/2 c. fresh lemon juice
2 T. paprika
1 T. white onion, finely minced
1 t. dried basil
2 t. dried thyme
1 T. fresh parsley, minced

1/2 t. salt
1/2 t. ground black pepper
2 T. canola oil
2 1/2 to 3 lbs.   boneless turkey medallions
nonfat cooking spray

In a medium bowl, combine the lemon juice, paprika, onion, basil, thyme, parsley, salt and pepper. With a wire whisk, slowly beat in the oil until blended. Place the turkey medallions in a glass pan and cover with marinade.

Refrigerate for at least 1 hour or up to 4 hours. Lightly spray the grill with cooking spray and preheat for 5 minutes. Place the turkey on the grill and cook for 4 to 5 minutes or until fully cooked and no pink remains. Serves 6.

NUTRITIONAL ANALYSIS:
Calories: 264
Total fat: 6 g
Saturated fat: 1 g
% calories from fat: 21
Carbohydrates: 4 g
Protein: 46 g
Cholesterol: 125 mg
Sodium: 294 mg

50 Great George Foreman® Lean Mean Fat Reducing Grilling Machine Recipes!

Grilled Chicken Legs with Latin-American Chipotle Sauce

1 T. canola oil
2 cloves garlic, minced
1 1/2 c. crushed tomatoes
2 T. dark brown sugar
2 T. molasses
1/4 c. cider vinegar

2 T. Worcestershire sauce
2 T. chipotles in adobe sauce
1/4 t. ground allspice
8 skinless chicken legs
nonfat cooking spray

In a large saucepan over medium heat, lightly brown the minced garlic in the oil. Add the tomatoes, brown sugar, molasses, vinegar and Worcestershire sauce, whisking to blend. Add the chipotles and the allspice. Whisk to combine. Bring the sauce to a boil and reduce the heat to low. Simmer, uncovered until the sauce is thickened, about 30 minutes. Remove any visible fat from the chicken. Coat the grill with the cooking spray and preheat for 5 minutes. Place one–half of the sauce in a small bowl and brush the chicken with the sauce. Use the remaining sauce for dipping. Grill the legs for 5 to 7 minutes, basting at least twice while grilling. Serves 4 to 6.

NUTRITIONAL ANALYSIS:
Calories: 148
Total fat: 5 g
Saturated fat: 1 g
% calories from fat: 31
Carbohydrates: 15 g
Protein: 13 g
Cholesterol: 45 mg
Sodium: 216 mg

Citrus Marinated Chicken Breasts

3 cloves garlic, minced
1/4 t. salt
2 t. dried oregano
1/2 t. ground cumin
1/4 c. cider vinegar

1/4 c. fresh orange juice
1/8 c. fresh lime juice
2 T. vegetable oil
1/4 t. black pepper
4 boneless, skinless chicken breast halves

NUTRITIONAL ANALYSIS:

Calories: 158
Total fat: 8 g
Saturated fat: 1 g
% calories from fat: 45
Carbohydrates: 5 g
Protein: 17 g
Cholesterol: 41 mg
Sodium: 193 mg

In a small bowl, mix together the garlic and salt to make a paste. Stir in the oregano and the cumin. Blend well. Whisk in the vinegar, orange juice, lime juice, oil and the pepper until completely mixed. Remove any visible fat from the chicken and place it in a sealable plastic bag. Pour the marinade over the meat and refrigerate, covered, for 1 to 2 hours. Coat the grill with the cooking spray and preheat for 5 minutes. Place the chicken in the grill and cook for 5 to 7 minutes. Serves 4.

Italian Marinated Chicken Sliced over Mixed Greens

3/4 c. white vinegar
1 T. sugar
1 clove garlic, pressed
1/2 T. fresh oregano leaves, minced
1/2 T. fresh parsley, minced
1/2 T. bay leaf, minced

1/2 t. salt
1/2 t. black pepper
1/4 c. extra virgin olive oil
4 boneless, skinless chicken breast halves
nonfat cooking spray
10 c. mixed salad greens, cleaned

In a medium bowl, mix together the vinegar, sugar, garlic, oregano, parsley, bay leaf, salt and pepper. Add the oil a little at a time until well blended. Reserve enough marinade for the salad dressing. Remove any visible fat from the chicken breasts and place in a sealable plastic bag. Pour the marinade over the chicken and cover. Refrigerate for 2 to 4 hours. Coat the grill with the cooking spray and preheat for 5 minutes. Place the chicken in the grill and cook for 5 to 7 minutes, or until fully cooked and no pink remains. Place the cooked chicken on a clean cutting board and slice into thin strips. Fill individual bowls with mixed greens and top with the grilled chicken. Drizzle the salad with the reserved marinade and serve. Serves 4.

NUTRITIONAL ANALYSIS:
Calories: 245
Total fat: 15 g
Saturated fat: 2 g
% calories from fat: 59
Carbohydrates: 6 g
Protein: 18 g
Cholesterol: 41 mg
Sodium: 351 mg

Strawberry-Lemonade Marinated Chicken

1/2 c. fresh lemon juice
1 t. lemon zest
1/4 c. frozen strawberries, thawed
1 t. fresh sweet basil, minced
1/2 t. salt

1 t. ground black pepper
2 T. vegetable oil
4 boneless, skinless chicken breast halves
nonfat cooking spray

NUTRITIONAL ANALYSIS:
Calories: 152
Total fat: 8 g
Saturated fat: 1 g
% calories from fat: 46
Carbohydrates: 4 g
Protein: 17 g
Cholesterol: 41 mg
Sodium: 337 mg

Combine the lemon juice, zest, strawberries, basil, salt, pepper and oil in a blender and pulse until smooth. Remove any visible fat from the chicken and place the chicken breasts in a glass dish. Pour the marinade over the chicken. Turn the chicken once to coat. Cover and refrigerate for 2 to 4 hours. Lightly coat the grill with cooking spray and preheat for 5 minutes. Grill the chicken for 5 to 7 minutes, or until no pink remains. Discard any unused marinade. Serves 4.

50 Great George Foreman® Lean Mean Fat Reducing Grilling Machine Recipes!

Spicy Asian Chicken with Chopped Peanuts

2 T. peanut oil
1 T. ground ginger
1 T. five-spice powder
1/2 t. red pepper flakes
1/2 c. green onions, finely chopped

1/4 c. low sodium soy sauce
1/4 c. rice vinegar
4 boneless, skinless chicken breast halves
1/4 c. peanuts, shelled and finely chopped
nonfat cooking spray

In a medium bowl, mix together peanut oil, ginger, five-spice powder, pepper flakes, green onions, soy sauce and vinegar. Blend well. Remove any visible fat from the chicken. Coat the grill with the cooking spray and preheat for 5 minutes. Place the chicken in the grill and cook for 2 minutes. Spoon the sauce over the top of the chicken and cook an additional 3 to 4 minutes, basting occasionally, until the chicken is fully cooked and no pink remains. Serve topped with the chopped peanuts. Serves 4.

NUTRITIONAL ANALYSIS:
Calories: 234
Total fat: 13 g
Saturated fat: 2 g
% calories from fat: 50
Carbohydrates: 9 g
Protein: 21 g
Cholesterol: 41 mg
Sodium: 583 mg

CHAPTER 6

Great Grilled Seafood

Fish and shellfish are easy to prepare in the George Foreman® Lean Mean Fat Reducing Grilling Machine. Fish and shellfish cook very quickly, however, so test the fish about 1 minute prior to the recipe suggestion so that you don't overcook the fish. Mild white fish will be done when it is opaque and flakes easily with a fork. Fish such as salmon and halibut are done when the fish flakes easily with a fork and the flesh is firm.

Inside this chapter you'll find exciting recipes for healthful family favorites. Try *Grilled Salmon with Lemon Basil Butter, Ginger & Orange Grilled Scallops* or *Coconut Grilled Swordfish.* When you want to experiment with various types of grilled fish, choose any of the following recipes that offer similar types of fish and grill for about the same length of time. Most types of fish are an excellent source of lowfat protein, so enjoy the full flavors of fish and shellfish without the heavy fat!

Grilled Salmon with Lemon Basil Butter

4 6 oz. salmon fillets
1 t. paprika
1 t. sugar
1/2 c. lowfat margarine

1 T. fresh basil, finely minced
2 T. fresh lemon juice
1 T. green onions, finely minced
nonfat cooking spray

Lightly coat the grill with the cooking spray and preheat for 5 minutes. Place the salmon fillets in the grill and sprinkle with the paprika and sugar. Grill for 6 to 8 minutes, or until the fish flakes easily. In a small bowl, blend the margarine, basil, lemon juice and green onions. To serve, arrange each steak on a plate and top with a generous spoonful of the lemon–basil butter. Serves 4.

NUTRITIONAL ANALYSIS:

Calories: 418
Total fat: 30 g
Saturated fat: 6 g
% calories from fat: 63
Carbohydrates: 3 g
Protein: 34 g
Cholesterol: 112 mg
Sodium: 234 mg

50 Great George Foreman® Lean Mean Fat Reducing Grilling Machine Recipes!

55

Salmon Fillets with Tarragon & Marjoram Marinade

6 4-oz. salmon fillets
1/2 c. fresh lemon juice
4 cloves garlic, minced
1/4 c. vegetable oil
2 t. fresh tarragon, minced

2 t. fresh marjoram, minced
1/2 t. fresh ground black pepper
1 t. salt
nonfat cooking spray

Place the salmon fillets in a large glass pan. Mix together the remaining ingredients and pour over the salmon fillets. Cover tightly with plastic wrap and refrigerate for 4 to 6 hours. Turn the fillets once or twice while marinating.

Coat the grill with the cooking spray and preheat for 5 minutes. Place the steaks in the grill and cook for 6 to 8 minutes, or until the salmon flakes easily and is cooked through. Serves 6.

NUTRITIONAL
ANALYSIS:
Calories: 295
Total fat: 21 g
Saturated fat: 4 g
% calories from fat: 65
Carbohydrates: 3 g
Protein: 23 g
Cholesterol: 75 mg
Sodium: 442 mg

50 Great George Foreman® Lean Mean Fat Reducing Grilling Machine Recipes!

Coconut Grilled Swordfish

1/2 c. lowfat coconut milk
1/4 t. ground cinnamon
2 T. light brown sugar
2 T. fresh lemon juice

1/2 t. salt
4 6 oz. swordfish steaks
shredded coconut for garnish
nonfat cooking spray

Mix together the coconut milk, cinnamon, brown sugar, lemon juice and salt. Place the fillets in a shallow glass baking dish and cover with the marinade. Cover tightly and refrigerate for 1 to 4 hours. Lightly coat the grill with the cooking spray and preheat for 5 minutes. Grill the swordfish for 6 to 9 minutes, or until the fish flakes easily and is cooked through completely. Sprinkle the shredded coconut evenly over the fillets to serve. Serves 4.

NUTRITIONAL ANALYSIS:

Calories: 261
Total fat: 9 g
Saturated fat: 3 g
% calories from fat: 33
Carbohydrates: 8 g
Protein: 34 g
Cholesterol: 66 mg
Sodium: 449 mg

Lemon-Lime Basted Mahi-Mahi

1/2 c. leeks, finely minced
2 cloves garlic, minced
1/2 c. cider vinegar
2 T. fresh lemon juice
2 T. fresh lime juice
1 T. sugar

3 T. lowfat margarine, kept cold
1/2 t. sea salt
1 t. ground black pepper
4 6 oz. mahi-mahi fillets
nonfat cooking spray

NUTRITIONAL ANALYSIS:

Calories: 216
Total fat: 5 g
Saturated fat: 1 g
% calories from fat: 23
Carbohydrates: 9 g
Protein: 32 g
Cholesterol: 125 mg
Sodium: 477 mg

In a saucepan over medium heat, combine the leeks, garlic, vinegar, lemon juice, lime juice and sugar. Cook until the sauce begins to thicken, stirring continuously. Reduce the heat to low and continue stirring. Whisk the butter gently into the sauce. Do not let the mixture come to a boil. When the butter is blended, add the salt and pepper. Reserve some of the sauce for a finishing sauce. Lightly coat the grill with the cooking spray and preheat for 5minutes. Place the fish in the grill and spoon some of the sauce over the top. Grill for 1 minute and baste again. Grill another 2 to 3 minutes, or until the fish is flaky and cooked through. Serve with a spoonful of the reserved sauce over the top of each serving. Serves 4.

Grilled Sea Bass Fillets with Banana-Mango Salsa

1/4 c. fresh lime juice
1/4 c. extra virgin olive oil
1/2 t. salt
4 6 oz. sea bass fillets
nonfat cooking spray

Banana Mango Salsa
1 large banana, cut into small pieces
1 large mango, cut into small pieces
1/2 medium honeydew melon, cut into small chunks
1/2 c. sweet onion, sliced to make thin rings
1 ripe tomato, diced

In a large self-sealing plastic bag, combine the lime juice, oil and salt. Place the fillets in the bag and refrigerate while preparing the salsa. In a medium serving bowl, combine the banana, mango, melon, onion and tomato. Allow the salsa to sit at room temperature for 1 hour before serving.

Coat the grill with the cooking spray and preheat for 5 minutes. Remove the sea bass fillets from the marinade and discard the marinade. Place the sea bass fillets in the grill and cook for 3 to 5 minutes, or until the fish flakes easily with a fork. Serve with a spoonful of the *Banana Mango Salsa* over each fillet. Serves 4.

NUTRITIONAL ANALYSIS:
Calories: 435
Total fat: 18 g
Saturated fat: 3g
% calories from fat: 37
Carbohydrates: 36 g
Protein: 33 g
Cholesterol: 70 mg
Sodium: 428 mg

Grilled Shrimp & Pepper Medley

1 red pepper, seeded and thinly sliced
1 green pepper, seeded and thinly sliced
1 small white onion, thinly sliced
1 t. coarse black pepper
1/2 t. salt
1 T. extra virgin olive oil

1 T. fresh lemon juice
1 t. lemon zest
16 jumbo uncooked shrimp, peeled,
    deveined, tails removed
nonfat cooking spray

NUTRITIONAL ANALYSIS:

Calories: 91
Total fat: 4 g
Saturated fat: 1 g
% calories from fat: 39
Carbohydrates: 8 g
Protein: 7 g
Cholesterol: 42 mg
Sodium: 334 mg

In a large bowl, mix together the peppers, onion, black pepper, salt, oil, lemon juice and lemon zest. Let stand for 10 minutes to marry the flavors. Lightly coat the grill with the cooking spray and preheat for 5minutes. Grill the shrimp for 1½ minutes. Place the peppers on top of the shrimp and grill an additional 1½ minutes, or until the vegetables are tender and the shrimp are pink throughout. Serves 4.

Ginger & Orange Grilled Scallops

1/2 c. concentrated frozen orange juice
1/2 t. ground ginger
1/4 c. orange marmalade
2 T. water
1/2 t. salt
1/2 t. black pepper

1 T. fresh parsley, chopped
24 sea scallops
1 navel orange, peeled and cut into thin
    slices
nonfat cooking spray

Coat the grill with cooking spray and preheat for 5 minutes. In a small bowl, combine the orange juice, ginger, marmalade, water, salt, pepper and parsley. Mix well to dissolve the orange juice and marmalade. Clean the scallops and place them in the grill. Completely baste the scallops with the sauce and grill for 4 to 6 minutes, or until the scallops are opaque. Watch carefully to avoid overcooking. To serve, garnish with the orange slices and pass the remaining sauce. Serves 4.

NUTRITIONAL ANALYSIS:

Calories: 208
Total fat: 1 g
Saturated fat: 0 g
% calories from fat: 4
Carbohydrates: 35 g
Protein: 17g
Cholesterol: 30 mg
Sodium: 448 mg

Creamy Tomato-Avocado Topped Swordfish

1 ripe avocado
1 ripe tomato, peeled and finely chopped
1 T. fresh lemon juice
1 c. lowfat sour cream
4 4 oz. swordfish steaks

1 t. coarse black pepper
1 t. salt
1 T. lemon juice
nonfat cooking spray

NUTRITIONAL ANALYSIS:
Calories: 308
Total fat: 19 g
Saturated fat: 7 g
% calories from fat: 56
Carbohydrates: 9 g
Protein: 26 g
Cholesterol: 68 mg
Sodium: 718 mg

In a small bowl, peel and mash the avocado until smooth. Add the tomato and gently mix to blend. Stir in the lemon juice and sour cream. Cover and refrigerate. Coat the grill with the cooking spray and preheat for 5 minutes. Place the steaks in the grill and sprinkle with the pepper, salt and lemon juice. Grill the steaks for 6 to 9 minutes, or until the fish flakes easily. To serve, top each steak with a dollop of one-fourth of the creamy avocado and tomato mix. Serves 4.

Index